Blount's Anvil

BLOUNT'S ANVIL

a novel by

Don Hendrie Jr.

Lynx House Press
1980

LYNX HOUSE PRESS
Box 800
Amherst, Massachusetts 01002

Portions of this book have appeared in different form in the following magazines: *The Iowa Review, Viva,* and *Panache.*

All of the Chapter Titles are by Bob Dylan.

The cover was done by Abigail Rorer.

Typesetting & design by Maggie Checkoway Howell.

Thanks to Bridget Culligan & Sarah McNamara for their assistance with the production of this book.

The publication of this book was made possible in part through a grant from the National Endowment for the Arts, a federal agency.

Library of Congress Cataloging in Publication Data

Hendrie, Don Jr., 1942-
    Blount's anvil.
      I. Title
      79-93196
ISBN: 0-89924-024-0 (paper edition)
ISBN: 0-89924-025-9 (trade cloth edition)

Printed in the United States of America.

First Edition.

BY DON HENDRIE JR.:

BOOMKITCHWATT
(John Muir, 1973; distributed by Lynx House Press)

SCRIBBLE, SCRIBBLE, SCRIBBLE
(Lynx House Press, 1977)

BLOUNT'S ANVIL
(Lynx House Press, 1980)

"Things burst, and the devil drives."

— J. Paul Getty

CHAPTER ONE

I met a young woman whose body was burning.

Los Angeles
April, 1970

SHE — blonde and thin as sticks, her hair dyed black — came
free from Terminal Island Penitentiary and went immediately
to phone her husband Nick Winnoe. She believed him to be
in New England, where during the two years of her prison
sentence he had surely kept up the old games and deceptions.
But now, more interested in his money than in his tricks,
Sylvia Winnoe wanted fare in order to fly herself and her
friend Bip Rattray from Los Angeles to New York City for
their scheduled rendezvous with Mungo Croquet, the man
who had abetted Sylvia's imprisonment in the first place, and
who now needed the two women for other activities — Sylvia
knew from his telegram — activities which might well land
them in the joint yet again.

Sylvia had one hundred government dollars in a leather
shoulder bag, and on her body she wore the clothing in which
she had been busted on the first of February, 1968, for at-
tempting to smuggle cocaine and marijuana into the United

States from Mexico: an amber corduroy skirt and a plain blue, overlarge workshirt. Her hair was fistful short, her complexion white as paper.

While Bip waited outside the phone booth in her boyfriend's yellow station wagon, Sylvia called Decatur Samson in Dallas; from this friend and associate of Croquet's she hoped to learn Nick's exact whereabouts, perhaps a phone number.

"Decatur!" she said into the telephone; her husky penitentiary voice.

"Who's that?" he drawled.

"It's Sylvia."

"Oh really . . . like Sylvia you don't sound."

She sent a light snort over the wire, and pitching her voice higher, said, "I'm out today, Decatur, I'm free. Bip too. She's been out for more than a month, and we have to go to New York. How can I get hold of Nick? He never wrote—"

"Shit," said Decatur.

"Hey, don't do that, man." Her voice lowered again. "I'm still in touch with the artichoke, you know," she said, feeling silly with the ancient code-word for Mungo Croquet.

Decatur laughed like some fool stage villain. "There is no heart, sister, no heart left," and the line clicked dead.

$99 left.

Sylvia folded the booth door and went to lean into the car for a talk with Bip, who was black and ample, with a head of Afro and an expression as detached as brick.

"Did you get it?" Bip asked her.

"It was that dumb Decatur, Croquet's manager." Sylvia sighed through her teeth. "The dork wouldn't give me the time of day."

Bip pointed a smooth finger at Sylvia's nose. "I told you, didn't I? People just don't appreciate being phoned up by ex-cons." She cocked her head and brought up a tremendous white smile. "They tell me the whole country's got bugged since we went in."

"Well, I can't find Nick by telepathy." Sylvia reached across the car and took a cigarette from Bip's purse. After

Bip had applied the car's lighter Sylvia blew a flat stream of smoke at her friend. "I hate smoking."

"Quit."

Sylvia slapped the dashboard. "Mungo knows where Nick is, goddammit," she said, but she had no idea where Croquet was either — only where he had claimed he would be two days hence:

> WHEN YOU'RE OUT COME TO NYC AND I SHALL USE YOU WELL. ALL ELSE IS YOUR OWN BUSINESS. FIND ME AT 18 PERRY STREET ON MAY DAY, AND BRING THE BLACK ONE IF YOU LIKE. ANON.
>
> MUNGO.

Bip said, "Maybe he'll send you a heavenly message through the ether," as if she didn't mean it particularly. "Come on, we're wasting time. I got to have this car back to Stanley."

"Why couldn't Stanley spring for the plane tickets?" Sylvia asked, knowing what the answer would be.

Bip laughed as she started the car. "He'd kiss a pig before he would do such a thing. But get in. I do have one idea in my feeble head."

Sylvia shrugged, flung the cigarette at the phone booth and entered the automobile, fairly certain that Bip's scheme would involve some complication of sex and the legally dubious. They crept into the great swarm of traffic, as resolute a couple as you could find on the Santa Monica Freeway that particular day.

In Benedict Canyon, Beverly Hills, you could see them ascend Stanley's drive, a way as convoluted as a marble shoot, as steep

as a shed roof. Bip shot them up the ramp and brought the
car's bumper within a foot of Stanley's weathered portal.
Inside, across the bricked floor of the nearly empty living
room, and out onto the sundeck that overlooked the dips
and whorls of the canyon, they discovered Stanley nude and
asleep. Sylvia gazed with interest and a certain amusement
at this specimen: wiry Stanley, a man of tawny skin and red
pubic hair . . . as vulnerable as a dozing whippet.

"Hey, white boy," Bip hissed, as if to lure him to some
dangerous assignation. Stanley cupped his bespeckled balls
and sighed through his slack mouth. Bip chuckled and looked
at Sylvia with a pleasured and wry face. "If you've been
dreaming about nekid men for two years, as I know you have,
this Stanley ought to about ruin those dreams. Hey, Sylvia's
here, wake yourself."

"Don't," Sylvia said, "I'll see him soon enough." She
liked the way his penis fell loose against one thigh, thought
it a decent way to reacquaint herself with the things. "He's
pretty. A damn sight prettier than old hairy Nick."

"He's just Stanley dreaming about himself. You want
something?" Bip touched the worn stuff of Sylvia's shirt.
"I know, you want a shower, you want a shower all by your-
self. That's the first thing I did when I came out. I said to
Stanley, Stanley you just hold on to yourself for a bit while
I go love that shower; just me and that water and no *women*
bespeakin' my fat ass."

Sylvia smiled and dropped her leather bag to the deck.
"That's the best thing I've heard since the matron told me I
better take care of myself out there cause if she saw me back
in she'd bite my ears off."

Stanley scratched, snuffled deep in his throat and threw
a forearm across his eyes.

"Come on then," Bip said. "I'll show you the facilities."

They went across the cool bricks and into a bedroom
that was furnished with a floor mattress and a stack of open-
front cubes stuffed with clothing and linen. Bip took from
one cube a lavender towel, tossed it at Sylvia, and indicated
a smaller room where Sylvia could see a dark commode and

a portion of the shower's sliding glass doors.

"You want some other clothes?" Bip asked as Sylvia began to undo the ties of her skirt.

Sylvia laughed. "Now what of yours could I possibly wear?"

Bip cuffed her cheek gently, words rising up from low in her throat. "You can have some of Stanley's pants." She grabbed a burgundy garment from another cube. "Here you go . . . and this strappy top for your woeful titties."

Sylvia dropped the skirt to the floor and kicked it up into Bip's smiling face. "Don't make fun of my breasts," she said, unbuttoning her shirt. Bip allowed Stanley's clothes to fall from her hands, then whisked Sylvia's skirt from her face and ripped the old corduroy in two as if it were newsprint. "Hey!" Sylvia cried.

"It's a new era, little sister. You don't want these shit-for-rags." Bip grabbed hold of the shirt even before Sylvia had shrugged it off of her back, and with a jerk Bip spun her out of it. In a moment Bip had reduced the thing to tatters. "Now them drawers and that brassiere," she ordered.

Sylvia backed off. She liked the game well enough, loved Bip as much as anyone, and appreciated that their new freedom meant they could play like this without fear of the dyke halo that Bip, in prison, had hated.

Sylvia reached for the center of her own back, elbows extended like wing stubs, and undid her bra which she hunched out of and dropped to the floor, still retreating in the face of Bip's joyful approach. Ignoring the flimsy bit of government-issue white, Bip came on, motioning with a regal palm.

"The drawers, jail-chick, give them here!"

Sylvia's back mashed against the door jamb. "You leave me be, Bip Rattray," she said, "or I'll snatch you baldheaded and take up with that pretty Stanley instead of your ugly self."

"You think so?" Bip stood over Sylvia in her tie-dyed shift; she grinned briefly as Sylvia bent at the waist, charged forward and buried her face in the pillow of Bip's belly.

"Ooomph," Bip cried, but she did not retreat. Her hands

ran down Sylvia's lowered back until the fingers slid beneath the weak elastic band of the underpants. In a motion as smooth as removing a child's bathing suit Bip's hands went over Sylvia's lean buttocks, emerged, and continued along her shanks until Bip, now bent over Sylvia's back, was able to secure a grip on her calves and swiftly come erect. So that Sylvia found herself upended, dangling, the drawers ripped asunder from the natural force of Bip's elbows.

Sylvia shrieked and knew a roaring of blood in her ears. A startling stream of cool air — the blessing of Bip's lungs — flowed over her parched private parts.

"There you go, darlin', you free now. Free at last!"

Bip lowered her friend to the floor, stepping backward in order that Sylvia might gradually, from neck to ankles, become supine on the keen bricks, as peacefully naked as ever she had been.

She looked down along the length of her body, past the brief nipples to the upper end of the rufous scar that ran vertically from the tip of her sternum to the arc of fair pubic hair. In the middle distance Bip's dusky feet were planted between her own.

"I can't move," Sylvia said. "Why don't we stay here? Right here in California. You, me, Stanley. I don't really want to go to New York, Bip; not for Mungo, not even for Nick."

"You're hooked, dear," Bip said. "Or had you forgotten that you're a married woman, a convicted felon, and probly still subject to dingus Croquet's funny powers? You still half-way in love with him, am I right?"

Sylvia rolled her head back and forth. "I could change my name, I could go someplace where they never heard of smuggling and outlaws and stupid stupid love."

Bip gazed down at her, at once gentle and harsh. "Lord, child, that Mungo wouldn't *let* you; he'd find you if you turned up a nun in Kathmandu."

"I suppose . . . " Sylvia drummed her fingers along the scar as if she were playing a recorder, summoning her men. If it hadn't been for Nick and never quite knowing when to take him seriously she would still have a spleen, and an un-interrupted body for whoever cared to have it. Suddenly, her life seemed too weary-making to imagine. "Well," she said finally, "if you really believe Stanley can help us make some money, then we'll just go along to New York, like the man said. Take it as it comes."

Bip appeared relieved at the change of subject. "I told you, Stanley's clever awake . . . and he's a weavin' spider in his business."

"Great, great," Sylvia murmured. "Now, love, please to put me in the shower and I'll temporarily wash away my sins and crimes against the state."

Bip stepped over Sylvia and into the bathroom.

In the shower, the water — an almost solid cylinder of it — fell against the back of Sylvia's neck while she washed with a sliver of Ivory soap. Momentarily her mind flew back to the prison showers, where deliberately shaped bars of this same white soap often served as lathered dildoes; as public a matter as brushing your teeth in front of the floor's forty women: the brief, rapturous spasm displayed. Not for Sylvia though, this particular activity. She bent forward, the water thumping her vertebrae, to cleanse her vagina, anus, thighs, calves, and all the crevasses of her feet. She thought of Nick (toe-sucker; swarthy angel of cunnilingus) and wondered idly but with a fresh twinge of anxiety for this man who was still her husband, where in the world he was. Was he still the public automobile mechanic? the secret writer of screenplays? And did he even know she was out? Had Decatur Samson perhaps called him after her own indiscreet call to Dallas? Told him his dope-smuggling wife had been sprung eight months early for near-impeccable behavior? She remembered bitterly Nick's last words to her, in Mexico, in Manzanillo more than two years ago: "If you have any trouble, Mungo will take care of it. He's a genius. No way you'll go to prison, Syl." A fool's words into her own foolish ears. And did Nick now feel, after all of this hideous silence, any obligations to her at all? Money, guilt, love. She doubted it. She was on her own, and elusive, maddening Croquet would be waiting in New York with instructions for her future, orders for the seventies.

$99 left, plus some change, and not a stitch of clothing to call her own.

Later, in the afternoon twilight of Stanley's living room, Sylvia — dressed as Stanley — met Stanley, who continued nude though now awake. Sitting cross-legged on the floor in front of the door to the sundeck, he seemed to be examining the follicles of his thighs, picking and flicking at imperfections, although Sylvia could see none. His face, no longer sleep-loose, was a model of regularity made slightly incongruous by a thick mass of red hair. She liked him: his slightness, and the way he concentrated on the details of his body with no apparent apprehension of her as she stood in his bedroom door wearing his burgundy pants and white tanktop.

Behind the brick half-wall that separated the kitchen from the main room, Bip was at work. Her hair glowed dusty-grey in the light from the copper hood over the stove. When she saw what was happening, saw that Stanley was unaware of Sylvia's presence, she called out roughly to him. He did not react immediately, but then slowly raised his face full at Sylvia, and smiled gently, perfectly. His eyes were hazel, perhaps too exuberant. Sylvia wondered if he saw her and she had a sense that he might be seeing what was not there, something gaudy and unusual; certainly not her frail self.

"Hello there," she said.

Stanley lifted one hand to the level of his chin, palm forward, and continued to smile. He narrowed his eyes, then made them go wide, as if he were trying to provoke a child to laughter. Sylvia found herself returning the gesture, or signal, whatever it meant; surely excited by this first ritual with a non-official man in two years. She moved toward him and was surprised when he leapt to his feet and stood with the faint tremor of a released spring, smiling still.

8

Not a jot of embarrassment: face, skin, flaccid penis poking like a red-haloed thumb from his groin, she noticed, though she continued to watch his eyes, still not sure what he saw.

Bip again called out from the kitchen. Again, Stanley appeared not to hear, but the smile drew down, the teeth went away and he looked only eagerly pleasant.

What the hell, Sylvia thought. She had listened to Bip talk about this fellow for a year and a half; he was no stranger, strange though he might be now. She stepped into his aura, put a white hand on either of his shoulders, and kissed him directly upon the lips.

Stanley sniffed. His lips were dry, taut, chapped, yet there was a taste of sweetness that Sylvia hadn't expected from a man who had been asleep in the sun — no sour grog of breath. His sniff seemed to dimple the flesh of her cheek, even though she knew she had only heard it. She drew her face away from his but kept her hands afixed to him, measuring the thinness of his width, this man, his ribs. Naked before her. Smelling — she knew it in a rush — of cocaine and Ivory soap.

"Mrs. Winnoe," he said, "I am you. Are you not me?"

The clothes, his clothes. She felt herself *behind* them; bagged like groceries in Stanley's fresh containers. And she was aroused, as Bip had told her would be the case with this man. Her calves tingled under the trousers. She removed her hands from him. He failed of reacting; he failed of everything except a demeanor that in its cocked stillness gave her pleasure, and she knew for certain that men had not gone from her ken.

CHAPTER TWO

Oh, where have you been my blue-eyed son?

New York City
May 1, 1970

HIS heart was no dark reeded cave today. Mungo Croquet.
Yesterday's telegram a glad bull upon the table:

> YOUR WOMEN ARRIVE TWA 1-4-8. FIRST
> OF MAY. 8 A.M. FLUNG TO YOU WITH
> LOVE. STANLEY.

Croquet costumed himself, a white caftan for the airport.
Who would look at *him* — a Shakespearian actor of regional
repute, a mild albino — in this city of United Nations? His
Friday morning journey was not to meet the two women, no
indeed, but merely to see them from their aircraft, to see
them in their bodies; to watch them embodied through the
air terminal corridors of machinery and clocks, past Security
in mufti or otherwise. He wished only to observe their

manner of landing, of walking with eyes fresh from prison ...
and, as always, to test his own power of simple disguise. His
will.

He would not answer the ringing telephone in this Green-
wich Village apartment. Nick Winnoe or Decatur Samson or
the unpredictable political gnomes could damn well wait until
he had made his journey and eaten a breakfast.

In the cab, which was commanded by a dwarf with me-
chanical leg-extenders like a vision of erector sets, Croquet —
his breath smelling of witch hazel — sat in bright dawn and
was driven into the neon day. Through a chaotic web of
concrete and copper and aluminum and coaxial connections
went Croquet, his eyes as silent as the moon, and when the
vehicle had brought him through the long arc, ARRIVALS!
ARRIVALS!, the upward ramp of macadam overlaid with
every morning's waxen and metallic debris, he alighted amid
a twirl of caftan, the driver already paid via-tray, and tipped
for that part of him which had never got to be; and Croquet's
arriving flourish was noticed by absolutely no one. You
could see him, though, pneumáticed into the airport, this
blanched mummer of a blue-eyed Othello.

In the terminal time was digital: 7:56

He swept along a corridor of gleaming maroon and es-
calated to a domed region of spacious walkabout, where
human clusters gaped at wall-hanging television monitors
which offered only a fixed schedule of one airline or another;
where others, individuals, sat like infants in high chairs watch-
ing the day's early shows on arm-mounted sets that leased
for the rate of twenty-five cents the half hour. In the center
of the concourse, young soldiers performed a yawning, un-
shaven promenade; and they *did* reconnoiter Croquet, as
though he were some tow-headed foreigner boldly entering
an exclusive NCO watering club in San Antonio, Newport
News or San Diego.

". . . one'a them rock stars," said a Navy corpsman when
Croquet had passed him by.

"It's that junkie from Abilene," his buddy explained.
"Micky Snow . . . Hey, Mick! How they hangin'?"

Croquet continued on.
7:59

Until, in striding toward the wide portal of a shop, one of a vast arcade —

GLOBAL NOTIONS

— he met himself reversed, on the bluish glowing face of the shop's closed-circuit television monitor which was hung from the ceiling by gilded links of chain. He stopped. He stopped. He walked into the environs of the shop. He walked into the environs of the shop. He stared upward at himself: the *he* who vertically bisected the screen, the notion counters and terminal background curving away to either side of this observing centerpole. Who could that gossamer man be? Croquet's attention fixed exclusively upon his electronic self; the 'real' periphery ceased to exist. A clerk hoofed into the scene on shoes that reversed her ordinary center of gravity. On-screen, Croquet spoke to her. "I'm just looking, thanks." Exit clerk. It was uncanny. He might conduct all of his affairs in such a manner, from such a throne as this. Here were the best duplication facilities: the self in two different places at once.

A rectangular clock occupied a portion of the screen's distorted rear-ground.
8:01

He felt himself to be a mannikin posted at the shop's entrance. Inert Watchman. Behind him (in front of him) the morning traffic glissaded in a fore-shortened parody of haste, all twittering legs, and arms held at impossible akimbo; thus the world passed behind (in front of) Croquet, and in the cave of his chest his gaming heart prepared itself for Sylvia, whose aircraft had accordioned with the terminal at eight o'clock.

Digital time has no seconds.
8:02

On-screen, a customer trotted from the terminal mass, traveled around him, then disappeared. His voice asked the clerk for an ordinary keychain. "You mean a plain one?" she responded. Croquet could *hear* the man's unvoiced impatience. "We don't have none. You want a rabbit's foot one?" The customer snorted and departed back into the roaring electronic dance.

8:04

He watched a girl, no, a young woman slice by the higher Croquet; the after-image — she was now gone from the screen — a shock of cropped black hair. Sylvia. His heart, invisible to the hidden camera, leapt. Her face appeared at the lower curve of the screen; she had faltered, was turning back to the Global Notions' realistic mannikin, but it was a movement so quickly arrested that Croquet knew she didn't know him. She withdrew. Success! In disguise he performed as a magnet, a pole for all but Her . . . who only wondered (he knew) why the man in the funny clothes stared so at the television monitor. He laughed silently and focused his chambered brain on the act of putting some magic into Sylvia's prison-ears: NOT TO FEAR IN NEW YORK, MY LOVE. So infatuated by the accomplishment of his ruse was he that he failed to note the entrance of the black one until it was too late, and Bip was upon him, on-screen and literally beside him, with a thick hand fixed to his elbow, whispering, "Croquet, you motherfuck, I'd know you anywhere."

He tried to keep his blinders intact by watching the dark balloon of Bip's head next to his own white space on the screen. Without opening his mouth or breaking the spell, he told her: YES. DON'T KNOW ME. SEE ME THIS AFTERNOON. And because Bip had always heard him so well, sometimes even obeyed him, she too went slicing away, and he could hear her speaking aloud to Sylvia and the clerk, "Baby, we've got to get you one of those Arab-type dresses right away; you can't go round New York in Stanley's duds."

8:07

13

Returned to his Hudson Street lair, Croquet left off the used camouflage and donned: a wig of straight auburn hair that fell over his shoulders like a mantle; a full, lip-covering mustache nearly russet in color; wide-wale corduroy trousers and a belt with a brass-encircled pi-sign for a buckle; an epauletted chambray shirt with flap pockets; and a street-worn pair of rawhide desert boots. No more the girdled albinic freak; now only a pale, spotless longhair in proper Manhattan uniform. This time he would answer the ringing telephone; the man in the caftan had had nothing to do with *talking,* had only been an arbitrary fixture of the greater global notion.

He ate breakfast, somewhat annoyed that the front strands of another being's hair kept dousing into his yogurt, but very soon he caught the woman's habit of maintaining his head erect, raising the spoon higher than was his usual custom. And for his mustache a linen napkin would do.

Promptly at eleven o'clock the ringing began. His salt water fish did not react, did not start or flash in their encrusted tank, did not care that Nick Winnoe would most likely be the man responsible for the noiseless wave vibrations within their perfect medium.

"Thomas Wicket here," Croquet declared in falsely stentorian tones; in name and manner this was how he always answered the Hudson Street telephone.

"Hello." Sure enough, Nick's hoarse gargle.

"How are you?" Croquet could hear Nick's breath over the circuit, could almost sense the pugnacity he wore like perfume. "I've seen your wife," Croquet said.

"Oh?" Gruff, interested.

"Yes, she's here in New York; came in this morning with Stanley's girlfriend. She seems . . . small, you know."

A silence too long. "Did she say anything about me?" he asked finally.

"No, she didn't. In fact, I didn't speak to her at all."

"Well, when you do," Nick said, "give her my best."

"I'll do that."

Nick sucked a breath and asked, "How was Dallas? I read somewhere that the cowboys were impressed with your performance."

"You mean Othello," Croquet said, laughing. "My Othello can murder the sleep of the most drunken of audiences. Where did you read about it?"

"You must be kidding," Nick said. "It's right here in the *New York Times,* under news of the hinterlands. There's even a picture of you looking like fuckin' Larry Olivier in blackface. How anybody can get away with it in 1970 is beyond me."

"Talent," Croquet declared. "The secret is to know that the play's an absurd melodrama, albeit bloody, with evil Iago upstage chewing on the ends of his mustache. Cackling lewdly and so forth. What do they say about me?"

"Nothing. You're the bloody melodrama," Nick said sharply.

Croquet recited with mock-sadness: " 'Every puny whipster gets my sword.' "

"What's that?"

"I'm glad to be back in New York," Croquet said, "although I had a good time with Decatur and he's promised to get me more work of the mumming sort."

"I hope it puts money in your purse, thick-lips," Nick said vigorously, apparently trying to change the subject and demonstrate Shakespearian savvy at the same time.

Croquet took a breath and continued in an altered voice. "Really, now, what about your wife?"

"What about her?"

"Shall I chain her to my sooty bosom, somehow? Or do you want to see her up there in Vermont, where you can give her your 'best' yourself, or what?"

"I don't know," Nick said. "Let her decide."

"All right, I'll keep her here for a bit of love's quick pants."

This was a game with them, of course, but . . .

Nick barked, "You're a slippery, no-account, and mercurial son-of-a-bitch, Cro—I mean, Wicket. You stay out of Sylvia's pants!"

"Easy," Croquet said soothingly. "It's not my fault you let her languish in prison without a word. I didn't abandon her."

"Fuck you," Nick said. And after a pause, "Let her bake off her pallor under your sunlamp."

Croquet couldn't resist teasing. "Stanley took care of that, I'll bet," he said.

"Yeah." Croquet could hear the pertinent synapses switching in Nick's brain. "I'm sure that's not all Stanley took care of. The cokehead has a nose for quim that won't stop."

"He has a nose for trouble."

"I don't want anything to do with him," Nick said.

"Oh? I thought he was going to do such great things with your scripts in Hollywood." Croquet began to shoot for the terminus of the conversation. "Let's not be stupid about this; Stanley can be useful, to you, to me, to Sylvia."

Nick was silent for several beats. "I guess," he said.

"Anyway, I'll entertain them here for a while. Anything else?"

"No . . . Yes. There's an interesting guy in town here, the sort of ally — isn't that the word? — you're looking for." Croquet made a sound of agreement. "He's a writer; doesn't have much to do with people. Christopher Blount."

"Blunt?" Croquet asked. "One of those novelists?"

"Right, but it's B-l-o-u-n-t. He wrote one called LOOSE ENDS and it's not too bad."

"Perfect," Croquet said. "Make friends with the man. Tell him lies, and if Maid Fortune blows up in our faces he can write a brief book about it. I think it's a wonderful idea."

"Yeah," Nick said. "I'll see him around."

"Play with him. I've got to go. Good-bye," Croquet called into the instrument.

"I trust I haven't dashed your spirits, friend," Nick said with heavy sarcasm.

"No, not at all. Goats, monkeys, winnoes, they're all the same. See you, Nick."

"Until that time, Mr. Wicket."

After noon Croquet took the elevator DOWN; he entered the stainless steel box with Gjertrud from the adjoining apartment. "Who are you today?" she asked, her hands and chest all luminous with camera equipment.

"Come again," he said with a faint drawl and a direct stare into her professional eyes; Gjertrud was a former bed partner and a continuing friend during Croquet's lighter moments.

"Tommy," she said, "you must be going to a poetry reading. No, too early. Don't tell me. . . uhh, you're going to observe the rally in Union Square against the Cambodian invasion."

"No." He grinned. "I'm going to see if I can persuade some very suggestible people to blow up the main offices of American Telephone and Telegraph, which, as you know, are right here in the Big Apple."

"Really?" The elevator whapped to a halt and the orange lobby invaded their colloquy. "How archaic. Now my idea of constructive violence—"

"Yes," he interrupted, saying yea-us, "but it's never too late for a good old-fashioned explosion, is it? I think the television masses need to be reminded graphically, from time to time, who's holding the bloody dinger."

They walked apace through the lobby. "The *dinger?*" she asked, somewhat archly, as if she were speaking to a precocious child, baiting him in a way that Croquet usually found both boring and flirtatious. "Whatever is that, Tommy?"

Croquet took her elbow and guided her outside, along the bleak afternoon sidewalk toward 12th Street. "You know what I mean," he said. "I have this image of a puffy leviathan with its gross snout on the destruct button."

"Oh bullshit, you and your silly rhetoric. Come on, seriously, what are you up to? Where've you been for the past month?" There was a plaintive, slightly possessive wind in her voice that Croquet didn't like. He knew she believed him to be a minor actor whose changing get-ups indicated he did a lot of fast hustling.

"I've been in Dallas."

"That's a nice place."

"Oh yes. It's lovely, and full of individuals with genuinely heavy thumbs."

She laughed politely as they passed a small park full of mothers and their children. A junkie or two. "Don't you remember?" she said. "I shot an album cover in Dallas last January."

"Gee. In tomorrowland?"

"I told you, it was the Mothers hanging every which way from the windows of the Texas School Book Depository."

Croquet tossed his auburn mane and looked hard at the almost-beautiful blonde woman who was as tall as he was, but all covered with supple brown suede. "Far out," he said neutrally. "That's a real contribution, Trood."

"To what?"

"Bad taste."

A wound; he could sense it broadcasting from her like a high-pitched whistle. As they turned up Eighth Avenue she appeared to be struggling for a grasp of his true feelings, if any. He stopped suddenly and, from a sidewalk peddlar, bought her a single iris.

She looked confused but said thank you.

"Someday," he said, "we'll let you photograph real life."

"Come uptown with me, Tommy."

He backed away from her, lifting graciously the corners of his mustache. "I never go up there," he said, "too many dingers."

"Dammit!" She stamped her foot. "What did you *do* in Dallas?"

"Othello. Turtle Creek Theatre Center. Samson Productions. Check your *New York Times* index."

She relaxed with the factual. A bus came up the street and stopped. "Anyway, that's great," she said, her eyes shaded against him with the hand that held the iris.

"You think it's great for a pale honky like me to pretend to be a high-toned and tragic blackamoor?"

By then she had climbed half-way up the bus stairs. The driver gave Croquet a mildly annoyed look. "I'm sure you could do it if anybody could," she called out. "Come see me, Tommy. Ciao."

Gjertrud was trundled off in a petrifying cloud of exhaust. Croquet continued on to Perry Street, walking thinly; the displaced air kept his hair back. Proudly, you would have thought.

The olive townhouse offered him a more or less blank stare, as though it were not only unoccupied but abandoned; the glass in the tall, narrow windows was covered over with visible soot and the heavy curtains behind the glass hung bedraggled and colorless. But it was certainly a rich man's house and it was certainly not Croquet's. The door at the top of the stoop, a double item made of mahogany, had been carved in high-relief: two griffons, one sly, the other gay.

Croquet was admitted by one of the anarchist gnomes, probably Sammy the Leaper, he thought — a kid really. Standing in the entrance to the parlor, its furniture draped and gloomily reflected in a huge mirror over the mantle, Croquet smelled dust and something vague but pungent, perhaps from Sammy's clothes: cordite or glycerin, some substance Croquet neither needed nor wanted to know about precisely.

"How they hangin', Sam?" he asked, remembering the morning's soldier, far away, a dream, a play he might have done in the early sixties. "Gentlemen of Idlewild." A smash.

Sammy's rimless eyeglasses struck opaque in the half-light. He shrugged and led Croquet through the hallway to the kitchen, where iron and ceramic paraphernalia lay about encrusted with gunk and general offal. Croquet sighed.

"Where's Elaine?" he asked, meaning the daughter of the owner of the townhouse.

"D'know. Meeting maybe. Lloyd's down basement." There was an echo of New Hampshire in his reedy voice.

"Doing what?"

19

Sammy looked irritated. "Making bombs, man, what else?"

Croquet grunted. "Do you think you guys could clear out of here for the rest of the afternoon."

Sammy shoved his hands into his back jean pockets and spun around once. "I just don't understand dilettantes like you," he wailed. "What kinda kicks do you get out of this anyway? Shit, don't you *know* Elaine's old man is coming back here Sunday? Like we don't have *time* to get out of here for the rest of the d-fucking-day."

Croquet stared at him and counted to five. "I'm just a gremlin in the machine," he said with avuncular precision. "If it's not convenient for you to leave, then how about keeping off the first floor, okay? Just tell Elaine that I'm bringing in some friends."

Sammy's glasses slid down the bridge of his nose; he twitched them back where they belonged. "You're the sugar daddy, Mister Silver," he muttered, using Croquet's townhouse name. "But not for long." He shuffled past Croquet and into the hallway to the front door, which slammed.

Small irritations.

Croquet went into the parlor to wait for Sylvia and Bip. As he took a seat in the draped wing chair he sensed that they were nearby, perhaps hurtling southward through one underworld tunnel, perhaps walking over the concrete; of course, it was a knowing based on no more than the likely, the obvious deduction, but still, Sylvia's sprung rhythm struck him with every other beat of his tuned heart. The pulses he was receiving reminded him of Mexico, 1968, when he had deliberately influenced Sylvia to leave Nick and perform an act that, without Nick's forcefield to keep her safe, had been both stupid and dangerous. But Croquet had taken a craftsman's pleasure in matching his powers to Sylvia's intentions, and as a result she had been able to improvise what seemed a brilliant Smuggler's Solution: first, make hollow the upright support pieces of a crude, greenwood loom purchased that day in the Manzanillo market; next, pack the controlled substances in cheap garden hose — the entire kilo of priceless cocaine, as

well as compacted marijuana (for ballast, was that the idea?)
— then, slip a length of hose into each of the four loom
cavities and seal with corks made of wooden dowel. Simple,
efficient, and foolish. When Sylvia and the disassembled
loom — strapped atop Nick's VW bus — reached American
customs across the bridge from Tijuana, the wood had warped
enough to spring the dowels and expose the precious hose to
anyone who'd care to take a stroll the perimeter of the
vehicle.

GOOD-BYE, SYLVIA, Croquet's fallible brain had sung,
OUR SHRINKING FROM YOU IS ONLY TEMPORARY. WE ARE
SENDING YOU THIS FRIEND, BIP, TO GUARD AGAINST BITTER-
NESS, TO KEEP YOUR HEART IN SYMPATHY WITH OURS, TO
LOVE YOU THROUGH THE SLOW WASH OF TIME . . . And now,
Croquet was sure that Sylvia came on toward him freely,
ready to play once again.

The doorbell. Here they were. He stood from the chair,
glanced into the mirror, smoothed his mustache with one in-
distinct finger, and then went to the great doors which he
flung open with a gesture both histrionic and gleeful.

"Stanley!"

"Is that you Edmund Silver?"

The man darted past him, disappeared, leaving only a
smudge of red hair impressed upon Croquet's left cornea.
Something was very much awry here; another rent in the
shoddy fibre of his will. He hurried down the hall, his heart
now full of vines, lichen, limpets; Sylvia's rhythm had been
choked off, gobbled up by this strange arrival. Only the
silence of the townhouse remained.

He called down the basement stairs.

"Don't come down here, goddammit!" A faint but
insistent voice; Lloyd's, he thought, not Stanley's.

A toilet flushed behind him, somewhere, in the kitchen
perhaps. He breathed deeply, turned, and walked back to the
kitchen where he stood in the doorway and waited for Stanley
to reappear. The toilet exploded again. He's running; he's
sick; his brain's burst from the coke; he's murdered my
women and tossed them in the river . . . Croquet thought,

but did not move for fear of finding out he was right. Never trust hopheads of any sort; they are mis-wired and usually out-of-sync. Croquet felt himself trapped in a state like Othello's final trance: Stanley-Iago behind the door with Desdemona's handkerchief, chortling epilepsy and jumble at the fair devil in the kitchen without.

"Stanley!" he shouted. "Come from there else I chop you into messes!" Othello's voice, right from the pit of his chest. Croquet knew himself absurd, gripped, his lines momentarily forgotten; stage center and dumb.

Before his eyes the bathroom door drifted open. Stanley, drying his hands on the handkerchief, no, a small white towel covered with asterisks, gazed upon Croquet with curiosity and no small measure of arrogance.

"Messes?" he said. "This kitchen's a mess, sure enough. These bombers are all alike, no respect for anyone's property. I tell you, Silver, I was in Herb Marcuse's apartment not so long ago and *his* kitchen was immaculate, spotless, a bloody monument to order." Stanley threw the towel over his shoulder and moved into the kitchen proper, taut, on his toes, his voice whizzing through the air as if dosed with helium. "Ay yi, I'm in jet-lag phase, got the trots you know, most wonderful trip though; I got a good story for you about the women. Where are they, by the way?"

Croquet decided he would be straight with this clown, until something hard and useable spilled and splashed at his feet. "I don't know where they are," he said.

"I like your mustache, gives a sort of startled look to your bleached visage. Humm, the girls, yes. They must be on their way, then, unless of course they've been busted or otherwise officially detained, which I personally would consider a major disaster, but these things happen; the times are just plain astounding, don't you think? and they've been leading rather dangerous lives of late.

"They nearly blew a coke deal in fucking *Bel Aire,* man. Yeah, that's right, that's how they got the dough to fly out here. This real sweetie named Liebling came over to my place in the canyon for maybe twenty grams. I wasn't there and

Sylvia had the audacity to suspect him of being a cop. Him! Can *I* help it if he wears brown shoes and his head is square? So, later, I made Bip and Sylvia go up to his place in Bel Aire with the goods; for this act I would give them a healthy percentage, of course. You can't just give women things. And when they got there — you won't believe this — Henry Kissinger was having a drink with Mr. and Mrs. Liebling."

"Stanley—"

"It's true, word of honor. Liebling acted as if the girls were canvassing for the ADA and gave them ten one hundred dollar bills for their trouble. And I'm not forgetting the pretty twenty gram glassine bag that Bip had the pizazz to drop into his hibiscus. Sylvia said Henry had nose-pores like—"

Croquet tossed a hand in the air impatiently. "But I don't understand why you're here," he said coldly.

"What? I'm damned if I know, except my house became sepulchral mighty fast after the ladies split. I mean, Bip is my salvation. Is there anything wrong with my being here? You are giving me the evil eye, Silver-fish, and this place gives me the heebie-jeebies, too, now that I look about me. You shouldn't mess around with these rad-lib types."

"Something is wrong," Croquet said, finally giving tongue to the knowledge that had come to him since Stanley flung into the townhouse. "I know they were on their way here."

"Hey, don't look at me. I put them on the ten o'clock plane, chief." Stanley a trifle too eager; something up his sleeve, perhaps, but Croquet's receptive-brain could hear nothing but white noise from where Stanley stood. "They put half of Liebling's money down for the tickets; I saw it myself, and very generous of me, if I do say—"

Stanley's honed features went through a brief spasm that only made stronger Croquet's unfocused intuition that the man was either lying or deliberately leaving some large gap in his story.

Pop went Stanley's knuckles. "Well," he said, "maybe they spotted you and decided to trick you or something, you know."

"When did you get in?" Croquet asked.

"Ahh, let's see." He flipped his fingers in the air; a feat of calculation would produce believeable numbers. "10:56 A.M., Eastern Standard Time, and that's the truth. Soon's I left the plane I went to the Men's Room. Happens every time I come to this canyon of shit."

"Then what?"

Stanley searched the ceiling for his itinerary. "I bought a newspaper and over a rather good prune danish confirmed my West Coast premonition that that slope-shouldered Tricky really was insane enough to invade a country on his own say-so. Then I called our friend Nick."

"Really? How's *he* doing?"

"You know," Stanley said. "I told him his latest script needed another rewrite before the producer would look at it again. He was pissed, like always, but he didn't say word-one about Sylvia, if that's what you're thinking. After that I came in town, then down here. Stood around a demonstration in a park, but when it started getting ugly I walked over here. Where I am now, sir." He seemed relieved to have got through his recitation.

Croquet fixed him with vehement concentration. MORE, SPIDER, GIVE ME MORE!

Nothing happened. A blank screen. Then, to Croquet's surprise, he began to receive a string of vague, muddled images like poor newspaper photographs; images that did not seem to come from Stanley — who had turned his back to forage in the refrigerator — so much as they did from Croquet's own imagination of what *could* be. The pictures floated in front of Croquet's retina like a daydream caught between the actual Stanley and Croquet's electrified greymatter. He saw a dark-suited photographer at work; the long lens of his camera was pointed at a restless and muttering crowd, at a particular section of the crowd, at particular persons: Bip and Sylvia being fixed, being made into an official, grainy photograph.

He just might have it!

Now he saw a white police van being loaded, randomly, from the same flowing and angry crowd; Bip and Sylvia, hands joined, shoved roughly into the van by a cop with the face of a child.

It was not impossible, not at all.

"Liverwurst," Stanley said with disgust.

But Croquet had gone, you could see; disappeared.

CHAPTER THREE

Well, Shakespeare, he's in the alley
With his pointed shoes and his bells.

New England
Spring, 1970

HERE, Christopher Blount lived in a small town with his family and his things. Though he was a college teacher, a novelist, and a lover to his wife, he had no friends. This had not always been the case, but now he found his wife and children sufficient enough; and he didn't seem much worried that his arrogance and pride had made him a cold and lonely man; for he did not know it.

Blount believed in the truth of the lie called silence, and in keeping quiet he thought himself benevolent, wise and fair. And because he believed he knew himself as well as he knew his books, he allowed no challenges to his right to remain mute in the face of any threatening events or persons. While his wife Sara had not challenged him once in the seven years of their marriage, other men and women had tried him time and again, but Blount always won.

On Saturday mornings after the first good melt of Spring he made a point of playing catchball with his oldest son Oliver.

A fragile, taut boy of six, Oliver's habit was to make a fierce run for the ball as it arced toward him through the air, but more often than not the ball went on by him and struck the seepy grass at the moment he seized his father's knees with a cry of "Je-sus, Daddy!" When Sary Leary Blount heard the climax of this ritual, she invariably cast anxious glances for the whereabouts of her other son Tom.

At the beginning of the month of April a new babysitter was hired. One film night — the Blounts were to witness a political suspense film in the neighboring town of Brattleboro, Vermont — she met Blount in the kitchen.

"Mr. Blount."

"Hello there."

"May I come in?"

"My wife is in the shower."

"I'm early, I love your kitchen, your pans. Are those artichokes?"

"I'll show you the children's bathroom upstairs. That's where they are, and the aspirin."

"Thank you. I'm glad to meet you finally. My friend says you exude something . . . refreshing in your classes."

"What was your name? Come through here, that's the telephone."

"It's Monica."

"This is the living room . . . and the stairs; the children's rooms are off the balcony thing there. It's like toothpicks, please don't let them lean on it. Sara!"

"I won't."

"Sara!"

"What's this?"

"Proofs, galley proof for THINGS BURST."

"I didn't even read the other one yet. I know you get off on words, but reading is so insular."

"It is? Sara, don't come out, Monica's here."

But already Sara was poised above them, behind the balcony rail. From below, for Blount, she appeared a pale elongation of nude damp flesh, her adept face crowning his immediate apprehension of crotch hair, fleshed navel,

27

the water-shrunk nipples. "Hello," she said to Monica, and placed one hand on the railing, the other on a thrusting hip. As Blount watched her bend from the waist, shifting a portion of her weight to the railing hand, he quashed the impulse to shout maledictions, and only then noticed that Monica's up-turned face was an agog study.

"I think your house is lovely, Mrs. Blount."

"Sara!" Blount cried, "You're dripping on us."

"Monica," Sara said, "come and help me with the kids."

Monica ascended.

Blount owned a 10-speed bicycle as light as a suitcase. When he wasn't writing or teaching or moving about the house, he rode the nearby hills with a ferocity not seen in games with Oliver, or any of his dealings with Sara. As soon as the weather permitted he would put on greying T-shirt and shorts, a pair of wizened cross-country shoes, and then pump and gear the machine over tar, dirt, gravel, until his thick body sweat enough to ward off the spring chill. In time, the bicycle's racing tires had worn to flattened ribbons, and in April he replaced them with a type more suited to the crude surfaces over which he covered such great distances. Distance was the challenge, and his sweat a victory over space and the involuted beats of his heart. Dogs did not chase him, but Blount feared automobiles, their fickle drivers, more than he liked to admit. He never cycled at night.

Eight miles from his house was a crossroads of clapboard houses and a boxy Congregational church, a point on the map called Bristol West. On any spring morning, after a breakfast of yogurt laced with honey — his best pedalling fodder — Blount could reach Bristol West in thirty-five minutes. It happened that his habit of drinking water from the tap behind the church caused him, near the end of April, to meet Pablo Eaton, whose duck pond, backyard dale and house adjoined the church cemetery.

Blount, who had turned from the faucet with an unpleasant sense of being watched, wiped his narrow lips and permitted the bicycle to rest against his groin while the man walked toward him from among the jumbled headstones. He trod barefoot over the clipped grass until he could speak without raising his voice. His hair was tied back with a red bandana and he wore a bathing suit, a wooly Mexican vest without sleeves, and a blonde beard which the bright sun could fairly disappear. His smile, a lip-curve and a squinch of pale blue eyes, contradicted both his costume and the pear swoop of his soft torso as it fell outwards to his waist.

"You're Chris Blount," he said, and in the answering silence put forward his right hand. "Pablo Eaton. I've seen you from my pond."

Blount touched the hand briefly; it was very dry, and hollow. He allowed the pause to lengthen until he felt sure Eaton would break off this barren meeting, but the man seemed determined to outwait Blount's rudeness, which was based as much on Eaton's appearance as it was on Blount's usual desire not to speak to or be observed by strangers. Eaton's blue eyes harbored neither guile nor amusement; they merely waited. Finally, resigned to chat, Blount tapped the bicycle saddle. "Do you ride?" he asked.

The honest bellicosity of the response quickened Blount's pulse. "No . . . I don't write shitty books either," Pablo Eaton had said.

On his return home Sara handed him a collander of lettuce to wash. The tap water fell onto the fresh leaves, skittering soil grains, an ant, mulch debris. "We'll have Monica again tonight," Sara said, and as she turned from the stove she caressed with a forefinger the tip of her tongue. "Will you pick her up?"

Blount agreed, although he had never done so before. Lifting the collander, he shook through the excess water, wrapped the lettuce in a dishtowel, and had made one step in the direction of the refrigerator when a clot of cottage cheese thrown by high-chaired Tom curded across the front of his cycling shorts. "Tom! . . . You little asshole!" And the child's shrieks would not cease, even for his whispered comfort, "Daddy's sorry, honey."

Late that afternoon Sara brought him three large, curling photographs. Blount put aside his bourbon, put aside the bulk of his galley proofs, and took the black and white prints in hand. Each one seemed to gloss a nude portion of . . . Monica. Surprised, he finally said that they were "nice."

"Do you like the one in the leaves?" Sara asked.

"Yes," he allowed. "She looks like you, long legs, high ass, short back."

Sara laughed. "It *is* me, love. Don't you see? It was taken from up in a tree at the Eatons' house. The leaves were freezing."

"Were they?" Blount sipped from his drink and gazed at another slightly bleached photograph of Monica's — he was sure this time — thrust hip bones, bones which bracketed a groin thatch marred by a negative scratch or a piece of straw. "Eatons'," he murmured. Only in the third photograph could he see Monica's face: the camera lens had peered upward from below her navel, so that while even the tiniest corrugations of her nipples were agonizingly sharp, her face framed above was slightly out of focus. "Eatons'?" he said again.

"Yes," Sara said casually, taking the pictures from him and smiling. "That's where Monica lives."

At six, Blount fetched Monica. He propelled his red sedan into Pablo Eaton's yard and halted it in the L formed by the house and ramshackle barn attached. At the bleat of his horn a thick-torsoed woman stepped from the dusk of the barn and squinted at him. He fluttered his hand against the windshield, the woman put down her bucket, the squint relaxed into what struck him as wide-eyed scorn, and she disappeared, sucked backward by the innards of the barn. Then Monica entered the car. "Hi, Chris." The jocose lilt of the babysitter's voice set Blount's stomach to trembling; somehow, somewhere, he felt he was being toyed with, and he supposed that if it had anything to do with Pablo Eaton, or the photographs, or the bucket woman . . . then the hazards were closing upon him at bicyclist speed.

In the bedroom Sara caressed his cheek. "Lovie, would you shave," she said in her imperious way. Blount, who following his nightcap had skipped rope for ten glorious minutes, decided he would also take a shower. "And don't use any of that damned witch hazel," she called after him.

For Blount, shaving was as sensual as, and certainly more private than sexual intercourse. The smooth glide of the blade over the lathered cheek gave him the momentary illusion that his tawny skin was not filagreed with pock and enlarged pore. After he stepped from the shower he performed this act, slapped on the witch hazel, and stepped outside to allow the April night to evaporate his small rebellion.

The Blount bed rested on thick stilts and reached, he knew in the darkness, to the level of his diaphragm. He placed both hands upon the mattress frame, hopped, and in the air rolled horizontal, so that he settled gracefully if heavily just parallel to his wife's long body. Sightless, he saw in his mind the smile of anticipation spread the width of her Irish mouth. He slowly filled his lungs with air and heard in his inner ear the ratchet sound of his bicycle's main sprocket pedaled in reverse. He awaited the initiation of the act, the game, the match; and was not fearful because he knew there would be no words impinging on him, as if for Sara and Christopher the contract of conjugal rights had indeed been written for mutes. Sara had agreed, had finally conceded, when he left a written message beneath her pillow: *Talk not in bed and I will fuck thee silly.*

He knew her shape was risen over him. The hand, two slender fingers, encircled his cock mid-way like a wedding ring of bone. Motion occurred, layers of flesh moved against each other, and the dark mass of her bent to him as he watched from above. Always this preliminary of hers had seemed to him a kind of anesthetized mime, as if he were a dummy to be stroked and mouthed into proper animation; but he had, of course, never said a word. Yet, to be sure, there was pleasure in her craft. As the warm perpetual motion of her head bobbed below his abdomen, he forgot himself and grabbed in his fists a hold on her fine brown hair.

Habit and the rhythm of her mouth told him, yes, it was time to reverse, to go quickly to the apex of her wondrous legs, to take his smoothed face there, to be himself at work in that outpost for a while. But when he went to go she violated all custom (and his own pronouncement) by saying, in a most ordinary way, "No, not that," and thus he did not go down, but rolled instead on top of her, and in between the cinching legs. With a deft hand and a tilted pelvis she aided in the abrupt transition.

For a while it was the usual. He knew what came when: the furious, the calm, the steady; a touch, a bite, the need for pain just so . . . but a haste was upon her. The fingers that spread over his buttocks seized and pushed and seemed to signal that she had gone ahead of her usual self, that her skimming above the heady maw of her own pleasure was far beyond even her muted breath-intakes, which rose in his left ear like a musical scale. And it was all over: the rhetorical thrashing of her head; the legs that would seem to snap his femur bones; the fingers that sought to mark his flesh . . . as he so carefully held himself in check above her, determined not to crush or hurt, only to give silent pleasure when needed.

And only then did his semen go into her lax body, like words onto one of his pages.

The next night, Thursday, Monica laughed at him, not because he was drunk or driving badly, but because his refusal to answer her silly questions about writing had apparently irked her to a point that Blount foggily considered impudent,

23-year-old teasing.

"So you're sort of an ironical socialist," she said, "whose books giggle at history."

"You're out of your little mind." He could barely keep himself from shouting.

"Pablo says the novel is dead-dead-dead. He says your first one, LOOSE ENDS, is private and self-indulgent, like jacking off."

"That is horseshit," Blount said, maintaining the car in third gear, the better to negotiate the strange carbuncles on the road's night surface. Were his driving glasses fogged? "Eaton wouldn't know good fiction if it rang his balls." Saying this, he immediately felt ridiculous.

Her laughter was mocking. "Yes, he's competitive too; he's got that *ball* thing."

"What does he do, this critic, this champion of moral art?" Blount mumbled as they coasted into Bristol West.

"He makes photographs of dead things. He likes decay. Sara thinks he's kinda careless but that his images are very ... direct."

Before Blount could query this opinion of Sara's he had not ever heard, the Eaton driveway loomed before him; he determined to stop the car and allow Monica to walk the distance to the shaded windows that appeared to glow yellowly from within. He imagined a kitchen full of slumped chattering mummies, and as this image flickered through his head his foot by-passed the brake pedal and the car continued up the driveway. A fear of being drawn upwards to the Eaton house overcame him, and he brought back his foot for a good sock to the brake. The seizure propelled Monica's head into the windshield with an awful thud. "Sorry," he said, the car still rocking on its springs. "What do I owe you?" Monica said nothing. Enough wisdom remained to allow her to go without payment for the night's services. "See you," he called out to her dark shape.

The next morning, Friday, May first, Blount fell out of bed, and made, because of his hangover-stupor, only a child's heartbreaking whap when he struck the floor. His flesh burned at sternum, belly and knee as he attempted the kind of orthodox pushup his reason gave as the purpose for his being cold-cocked on the floorboards. But when he discovered his reflexes were no good, and that the cells of his brain were aswim with fusel oil, he let himself lie in the pulsing thump of his own misery.

In the bathroom, in the shower, he adjusted the water to a heavy stream on the back of his neck. To clear his brain of a certain regret — last night, after taking Monica home, he had boorishly refused to accompany Sara to bed — it was necessary to con it into ticking over properly. *Have mercy, Lorna Doone,* he recited until the sub-vocal words from his childhood got one with his heartbeat and the steady battering of the water on his lolling neck. Once the litany was established, it lasted through the toothpaste, the shaving cream, the blade, and the final slap and tickle of the witch hazel . . . when he found himself thinking not of the past, but the day ahead: food, sunlight, sweat, writing. Blount left the bathroom with his pain very much to the rear of his head.

From the kitchen window he could see Sara bent low over her garden's crooked aisles, Tom digging beside her in the unplanted dirt. Twelve o'clock. Oliver's lovely brown eyes rose above the window sill in front of the sink. "Daddy, Mommy says there's no yogurt, go get some, and hamburgers."

As a bicycle ride, the trip to the Windsor grocery store and back was a mere two miles, but Blount, by choosing to remain in the highest gear, made a hard, muscle-pulling game of the journey. He rode correctly, his shoulders almost touching the low handlebars, and with some pride in the ability of his ass to cleave to the polished saddle blade. On the way home, his knapsack hefty with meat, butter, bottles of wine, a newspaper, and the hamburger buns Sara had called for as he rolled out of the driveway, Blount came near to dying.

By accident most absurd. At the crest of the hill above Fellows' Orchard the blacktop narrowed; it was a stretch where he habitually slowed because of the squeeze situation that could result from a coincidence of cars going both ways, plus himself. Now, he looked over his left shoulder, and above the knapsack caught a quick glimpse of the cab of a maroon pickup. Squeeze right. Coast. In front, coming up the hill in the left lane, a cream Land Rover at a high rate of speed. No problem. He would listen to sprocket clicks until the shock of air from the passing vehicles signaled him free and clear. But the pickup, gunning and caterwauling, decided to pass him just as the Land Rover drew even with Blount's front tire. The result had been in his dreams; with the pickup's hot nose in his periphery, surely about to touch him, he wrenched the handlebars to the right, as if he were opening a stubborn valve, and was immediately upon the loamy shoulder, the bicycle bucking but controlled until its momentum fetched it up against the concrete edge of the Fellows' driveway. And he lost to the driveway and the weight of his knapsack. The concrete smacked Blount far more effectively than the morning's bare oak floor.

"You're all right?"

"Yes, thank you."

Jeffrey Fellows lifted the bicycle from his trunk and allowed it to lean against Blount, who held the wine-soaked knapsack by one strap. To prove to Fellows that he was indeed recovered from his spill, Blount turned and extracted the mail from his roadside box. The bicycle, without his support, fell to the gravel, the sound meeting his ears only after he had seized the packet of letters.

"Shit," he said.

"I'll be going," Fellows said.

"Yes, thank you."

Blount retrieved the bicycle and wheeled it up the driveway and into the garage. As he crossed the enclosed porch to enter the kitchen he spotted Sara in the backyard. Wearing a crocheted bathing suit, she lay with her bare midriff in the grass. She was reading the galleys of THINGS BURST, staring at his words through enormous black sunglasses. He put down the knapsack and went out to her with letters in hand.

"You get faster every time," she said without looking up.

"It's a matter of fanaticism. Tom asleep?"

"Umm . . . Chris, the women in this book are *bosoms;* they're unreal."

But Blount wasn't listening. He was reading his mail. "Cocksucker," he hissed, automatically.

She glanced up. "What happened to your shirt?"

"I fell. Look at this."

"What is it? There's blood in your ear!"

"Your friends the Eatons have sent us an invitation," he said, attempting to minimize with his voice both the seriousness of his ear and his peevish feelings about the small photograph he held: an image of — what? he wondered — stained languor. It was of a woman lying at ease on her damask couch, wearing coolie pajamas of white cotton; she smiled invitingly at the camera with a set of black-edged teeth, these beneath darkened eyes and a thick clout of Gibson-girl hair. In the hot sun Blount hunkered by Sara's head to point out the tiny nipple that blemished the woman's studiously arranged pajama top.

Sara shrugged. "I've seen it before. It's 'The Photographer's Wife,' made by Corsen in 1914." She pushed the sunglasses to the tip of her nose. "It's an invitation?"

He flipped the damned thing and read her the scrawl. "'Come cook with us May Day. Pablo/Lucia/Isolda/Monica!'" Blount had completely failed to keep the pissed-off tone out of his voice. "Christ, that's today," he finished weakly.

Before Sara could begin scolding him he retreated from the yard, withdrew to the safety of the bathroom to lave his ear and attempt to regain a better sense of this day. But Sara trailed him. Trapped. He felt that her very navel watched him as he douched the encrusted blood from his wretchedly scraped ear.

"You fall a lot," she noted wryly. "Are you starting to stumble and froth like one of your characters?"

Blount attempted a baleful look at his wife, but his

newly opened wounds disallowed it; he clutched at the sanguine washcloth and suddenly wanted desperately to work, wanted to go alone to his workroom and write down the sentence that had just now bled into his abused brain: *I've never told you this, but she had to taste herself before she could come.*

From upstairs Tom shrieked the end of his nap. And Sara was no longer with Blount. She called out from the stairway, "I'm going to Eatons', are you?"

Yes, one taste and she'd be gone.

"No! No!" Blount shouted. "I've got fucking something else to do!"

There was nothing ambiguous about her [he typed, in the workroom]. *No; my wife was more or less a complete lie. Her other lunacies surrounded me like puling kittens. She read Anaïs Nin, all of it, and went around saying, "I have to discover my lesbian self." I couldn't stand it, the foolishness of her horrible declaration. Where would she meet that self? In secret societies? Art galleries? A church? That was it! She'd taken her first screwing from a Catholic priest in a thunderstorm on Long Island Sound, and now she would get even with Holy Mother Church once and for all. This was my wife! Finally, I had to follow her, skulk after her wherever she went . . .*

Blount knew something was amiss with his bicycle's derailleur before he had gone one mile from the house. The chain would not hold on the high sprocket, kept slipping down with a rude clunk. He would lever it up, only to have the same cursed slippage occur again and again. He soon settled for the lowest gear, the hill-climber, and had to spend vast energies to transport himself the first four miles to Bristol West. The sweat was on him. So much so that despite his angry haste he stopped halfway up Dummer's Hill, dismounted, and walked the ailing machine the remainder of the grade.

At hilltop, after leaning the bicycle against a scabby maple, he finally asked himself what the fuck he was doing. He had needed at least a peek at the very picnic he had earlier denied himself so that he might pursue an embryonic fiction he barely understood; he had wished for a real tableau of children and outdoor cooking to replace the confusion of images in his head. But now, reasoning at speed, he knew himself to be on a fool's errand of mistrust. Sara could do what she pleased, *would* do what she pleased, and Blount was damned if he'd ferret out any secrets that he might have to nurse — hidden defects which would someday cripple him.

So, he took up his bicycle again, crossed the road, and prepared for the easy coast home, to the workroom, where he truly belonged, where the artificer's world in which he had to survive lay waiting to be stitched and hammered together.

As he poised, about to push off, he was delighted to see the maroon pickup take the curve a quarter of a mile below him. He heard the engine cough with the grade and he knew the truck could be stopped. His body tuned for the kind of solid confrontation he never would have found at the Eatons' picnic. He chose to simply sit and observe what would happen when the pickup's driver realized whose will commanded the heights. It came on, to the point where Blount could make out the general thickness of the man at the wheel, an impression of swart — in hair, skin, clothes. Perhaps ten feet in front of Blount the truck halted with a deep, frontal dip and a hollow tapping of slowed valves which ceased even as Blount saw the driver lean from the cab with his clumsy and pitted face arranged in a country-confident smile, as if he were about to render aid.

"Afternoon," he said, pushing at a black forelock.

Blount nodded politely but he had already measured his opponent; had observed his hands to be as small and unwieldy as dill pickles and covered with grease like a pair of gloves.

"Will it be acrimony? or will you let me apologize for putting you on your ass earlier?" The man spoke in such slipped and bitten syllables that Blount scarcely captured the words.

"What?" he said.

"I said I'm sorry you ride that thing so in-ept-ly."

Blount, who had the odd sensation that he was looking at an older, hulking version of himself, decided both that the apology was genuine and the man likeable. Blount nipped at a thumb nail, spat gently, and fixed his eyes on a point dead-center the man's low and smile-wrinkled forehead. "Do any sports?" Blount asked, consciously baiting.

Came a guffaw. "I just watch. Oh, I did play a little football out in California, before the pansies took over. You, you look pretty formidable there, with your skinny legs and your chest blown up like a goddamn trapeze artist."

"Do I? Well, get out of the truck and let's have a look at *you*."

"I know about people like you," he said, "but I *like* watching my body rot. My name's Nick Winnoe and you're going the wrong way. Pablo Eaton told me if I came out this afternoon I'd get to meet you."

Blount allowed the bicycle to roll forward until he was even with the pickup. "Look buddy, Nick," he said softly, "I'm only out for a spin . . . and you don't know a mother-fucking thing about me."

"You looked peakéd. I know that."

"Car coming."

Nick looked pleased. "Come with me. Drinks, burgers, get to know the folks."

"My family's there," Blount said thinly.

"I know it. Come on, prove you're not the misanthrope they say you are."

"You're irritating enough to make me do it."

"Ha! Throw your bike in the back. I've captured me a rare novelist."

An automobile full of sullen longhairs edged between them.

Lunging down the road to Bristol East, in the cab with cheerful Nick Winnoe, nervous of his bicycle loose in the pickup's bed, determined to protect himself from whatever

Eatons' might offer, Blount accepted a Camel cigarette from Nick's crimped pack. They smoked, jiggled.

"How you like Monica?" Nick finally asked, as if Blount was a hitchhiker to be queried about the weather.

"She's okay," Blount allowed, "but she's got the brains of an anchovy."

Nick hooted. "Come off it. She's got a swell ass."

Despite himself, Blount smiled. "That too. Are you married?"

Nick frowned, pondered, drove. "Marriage . . . Sometimes, yes, Sylvia shows up for a taste of it, a quick diddle among the tools. But mostly, she's away."

Blount felt impatient with the vagary, and he hated pulling teeth, but he kept it going with another question simply because he enjoyed listening to the man talk. "You're some kind of mechanic then?"

"Yes, I work down at Alvin Marsh's garage, and have for a couple years. Jesus, you must go around with blinders on."

"I just don't go to Marsh's," Blount said, and stubbed out his cigarette.

"You probably oughtn't to," Winnoe crowed, "I'm the worst mechanic in the whole state."

"I can believe it," Blount said.

Beside the Eaton house a yard of scaggy grass sloped down and away to the sudsy duckpond and the cemetery beyond. Children, including Blount's own, played near the pond. No adults in evidence as Nick drove up the driveway and parked between Blount's sedan and what was probably the Eatons' spattered van, all three vehicles arrayed before the barn door where Blount had glimpsed the bucket woman . . . Lucia Eaton, no doubt.

Monica came from the house before the two men could alight from the cab. She moved quickly to Blount's door, joggled it open, gripped his elbow, and said, as if identifying some edible root, "You, Christopher." Her fingers dug shamelessly at his ulnar nerve, so that he was drawn out onto the ground in order to alleviate the unfamiliar balance of pleasure and pain. "Great you came, fantastic." Rubbing his elbow, Blount was not inclined to believe her, yet she did seem genuinely pleased to see them both. Nick appeared to know her well enough to leer obviously at her haltered torso as he came around to receive her chaste kiss. "Hi, Nick," she said. She herded them toward the side door of the house like children being babysat. He felt manhandled, vaguely trapped, but he was, after all, here, and perhaps had something to learn of this house and its inhabitants. If the situation turned out to be more chaotic than he deserved, he could always take his family and leave.

They entered a drop-all foyer of bare sheetrock, linoleum bulging and waving over a floor strewn with broken-down toys, boots, kibbled dog food; and almost fell over a crudded child's swimming pool just in front of the kitchen's mouth. Through which they stumbled and discovered the bucket woman slicing an onion in the midst of the most incredible mess Blount had ever seen.

"Hi," she said vacantly, the tears carpeting her high cheeks like sweat. "I'm sorry," and she offered a whole-body shrug as commentary on the living kitchen. She had no breasts, nothing swelled but the nipples beneath her shirt. "I'm Lucia, Chris."

"Hello," said Blount, pulling from Monica's grasp and wishing the tears did not boil so from Lucia's eyes.

Nick traipsed through the debris on curiously graceful legs, not thick trunks as Blount would have supposed, but narrow stems topped by flapping folds of soiled blue jean over a non-existent ass. He made for the counter on which stood a crowd of half-gallon whiskey bottles, glasses, and what seemed to be the butt of a holstered pistol. "Blount," he called, "what will you have?"

Before he could answer, Monica turned on him, a forefinger just coming away from her tongue. "So why'd you change your mind? We thought you'd stay home with all your ironies in the fire."

He flinched. Lucia giggled nervously. "Nick ambushed me," he said. "I'll take a beer if you have one."

"Pablo's outside," Lucia explained, approaching the refrigerator and opening it on what Blount first saw as an underwater mass of seaweed and greenish creatures. A bottle of beer fell to the floor, an event Lucia seemed to accept as ordinary. Monica went for the bottle, had it opened and into Blount's hand before he could move.

"We should go outside," she said. "The kids are probably drowned."

For a moment Blount's stomach enveloped his heart. "Isn't that where Sara is?"

Lucia answered quickly. "The kids are fine. Issy's a big girl."

Slightly relieved, Blount quaffed a good portion of the beer, and as his eyes came down from the ceiling he noticed that Monica's long throat was covered with a pink flush that extended in amoeba patches even to the fair expanse of skin showing above her halter; it was the sort of gentle discoloration he had always understood to be the mark of successful sexual intercourse, but which Sara's body stubbornly refused to exhibit. "But where is Sara?" he asked again.

Monica smiled and put a hand to her throat to cover what was probably no more than a spring allergy.

Lucia moved on heavy legs back to her vegetable table. "Sara must be out back," she said.

"Let's go there then," Blount suggested.

Nick rattled his drink, Monica's fingers glided over her splotches, Lucia sliced a tomato with a knife like a razor. Blount felt some reluctance among them all to respond to his practical words.

"We do need a fire," Lucia said.

"Outside then, the outside is where we'll go," Nick pronounced, leading them — all but Lucia — through a battered dining room and a hallway hung with impeccably mounted photographs of what struck Blount in passing as a series of macabre, leathery mummies.

Outside, with the exception of the three children by the distant pond, they encountered no one. A black hibachi squatted by the grass near the stoop, beside it a bag of charcoal and a can of naptha. Now the shouts of the children came clear over the length of the ragged lawn, and Blount suddenly startled himself with a perfect, rational milli-second of explanatory image: the faceless, turgid form of Pablo Eaton simultaneously — triple-exposure — in fornication with the three women presently in his home. Monica, Lucia, Sara. Of course! All explained; conjecture erased. For Blount, in the thrall of this simple solution, all that remained was to do quick violence to Eaton, and then he could take his family home, away from this slough of flesh and mummery. Sara could be dealt with later.

But Sara stood beside him, bearing a platter of livid meat patties. "Hello, love," she smiled, "couldn't work?" Her breezy assertiveness, the very mundaneness of it, drove the neat epiphany from his head, reduced him merely to Sara's husband, nodding at his wife . . . as if he had been discovered storing his nosepickings beneath the arm of her favorite chair. *Her* neck displayed no amoebic blushes.

Sara gave Nick a friendly, familiar greeting, and brushing past Monica laid the meat beside the hibachi.

From behind them, from the doorway, Lucia said, "Pablo must be looking for the goddamn dog."

Tom chugged up the hill from the pond. "Oliver shooting ducks," he said. Sara laughed. Blount, watching her, watching Monica, and the child between them, decided that what he wanted most was to talk with Oliver, or at least to see what the boy was up to. He strolled away from the adults.

Next to the girl Isolda, Oliver was using a long bent stick to fend off one of the pond's plump ducks.

Blount took a certain pleasure in his own immediate irritation. "Oliver!" he shouted.

The boy turned quickly, his eyes wide and glistening. "Daddy, look, this duck's crazy!"

"Leave it alone. You're hurting it."

"But it's fun."

Isolda smiled, gap-toothed. She grabbed the stick from Oliver and scampered away through the mud.

"She's nuts," Oliver said. "She gave Tom a dog turd." His giggling made Blount's teeth ache.

Pablo Eaton stood across the water, perhaps fifteen feet from Blount. Same bathing suit, vest, same beard disappearing in the sunlight. "Chris," he said and waved his arm in casual salute. "Have you got a drink?"

Blount nodded, exaggerating the motion, unwilling to begin some conversation over the brackish water. He told Oliver to go up to the house.

Eaton began to amble the perimeter of the pond, blonde head lowered, possibly watching the lazy jactitation of his stomach. Blount went to meet him half-way — thinking to offer the bastard a chance to redeem his shitty books remark.

Once again they shook hands, and again Eaton's hand struck dry and hollow. "I'm glad you could come," he said. "We were thinking Sara a widow."

"Nick persuaded me."

"Did he? Let's walk by the graveyard. That fire will take a while."

Blount glanced up and saw that Nick and Monica stood distorted by the hibachi flames.

They walked through a stand of maples that bordered the gathering of worn tombstones.

Eaton said, "My idiot dog Jep likes to eat rocks. He once bit a chunk out of Elmer Moody's stone there. Granite is his favorite."

Blount snorted graciously. He wanted to return to the house, another beer, the safety of children, people, the Eaton mess. In him there existed no desire to chat; anything but to be alone with this relaxed, soft-bellied enigma.

"My property ends here," Eaton said, the emphasis upon the word "my." He stamped his bare foot down hard on an invisible line that only he could see in the grass. "I'm going to tell you something, Christopher. Unsolicited information. Maybe you'll put it in a book when you get home."

Blount stared at the man. The face was composed, even

gentle, you would have thought, yet did the thin nostrils not seem pinched, even whiter than the rest of his skin? And solemn blue holes for eyes.

"Man, Monica is balling your wife."

In the silence that followed, Christopher Blount knew he had indeed got the unwanted knowledge that was part of coming to this place. While his brain went about the necessary adjustments, it saw fit to produce frozen, tender images of the two women in all of their attitudes. And, finally, Blount believed that he would never utter about it a solitary word.

I've never told you this, but . . .

CHAPTER FOUR

The pump don't work 'cause the vandals took the handles.

New York City
May 1, 1970

"I'VE never told you this, Mungo," Sylvia said, in his apartment with the fish and the silent telephone, "but in prison I used to think it wouldn't be long before you would swoop into my cubicle like a condor and carry me off. It was all right that you set it up for Bip to be there instead, but at the time I felt adrift, as if you had dropped me in water churning and bloody with stupid fish, and if I didn't act just as stupid as the rest of them I'd be beaten about the breasts until they were black and blue. And let me tell you something, you won't get close to androgyny until you've grown yourself breasts and had some dolt slap them around for five minutes. Pain. I know pain is what you wanted Bip to protect me from, but the physical stuff never really got worse than the *noise* — the incredible din from six in the morning straight through to midnight. And in the midst of it you were allowed to practice two emotions: approval or disapproval. If you disapproved of what somebody did or said about your fancy college-girl vocabulary you better damn well be ready to defend the disapproval with your teeth and fingernails. See them. I bet you never saw me with anything more than boy nails before, but now any one of these could peel a peach. Sure, it's phony toughness, but you know better than most people how pretending becomes the thing itself. I know you know.

"You can see and hear how much I've changed in two years. You think I can't hear the sound of my own voice? It's like their *food* made my vocal cords stiff or metallic or something. From inside myself I have a sense that my skin's been treated with alum, some shrinking agent that makes me not quite fit myself anymore. It's as though somebody cut off my natural metamorphosis and just generally queered the process. I know all about it; I've kept track of every stage along the way.

"When I was nineteen and met Nick I looked like a sweet blonde butterfish. My calves were thick enough to worry about, and my breasts made Nick goggle and perspire. I could ring his ears with them, I could, and then one night I fell off a bridge. You know? Jumped is a better way to say it. Falling in California. We were on Route 1, right in the middle of that long curved bridge by Deetjen's Big Sur Inn, throwing firecrackers. Can you imagine Nick tossing cherry bombs into an abyss and giggling like a maniac at the explosions? Of course you can.

"We were both drunk and stoned, celebrating that we were about to be married. Then a car came flashing up the highway. It lit us. Nick yelled something and we went to opposite sides of the road; he vaulted the guardrail and stood on a kind of white scaffolding that was there, but I stayed on the pavement and saw him smiling at me across the way. It was that Winnoe smile, all crude and white, and his otter hair hung down on his forehead, and everything about him repeated the old refrain, Watch Me! He jumped backwards off of the scaffolding, still smiling. By that time the car was past and there was no danger, if there ever was any; I just looked over my own railing and when I saw what looked like grass I

47

jumped. The slope I had expected was not there, the grasses were the tops of trees, and I fell a long way.

"Not Nick though. Naturally. He'd only leapt to the ledge he could see clearly below him, and had assumed the same ledge was below me.

"I wake up in the hospital, a white white hospital in Carmel or Monterrey, and I feel so good I hardly notice Nick or the vague patch of pain at my left wrist. But I know immediately I'm clean and rested, wearing one of those open-back tunics, pale yellow. Then, whoops, I see the fat cast on my wrist, but that's okay since I feel so *sound* in all my other parts, at least until Nick tells me that I'm missing one spleen, a half of a kidney, and two days of time since I jumped. When I shout at his dark face that I don't believe him, he pulls away my tunic until I can see the bandages nipped all over my stomach, tits to bush. You see, see what a good job they did; it looks like a professional makeup job. Don't touch! Mungo. I feel twinges inside.

"At about the time I recover from the shock of the bandages I notice that my *body* is about half-gone, I mean diminished . . . the flesh has melted off of me. I'm a twig there on the bed. I've become — as Nick loved to say later — an ectomorph after twenty years as a certified mesomorph. It's all out of my control now; my hormones screwy and weird; there's no way back, no way. For two weeks I lie there. Nick's friends pay mournful visits. 'Far out,' they say, to a man. One of them brings a secret love message which explains to me that since I'm obviously a totally different woman, since I even *talk* differently — probably faster — I ought to get rid of Nick and be with him instead.

"Back up at college I had to buy all new clothes, nothing but corduroy and denim. I couldn't go to their nattering parties anymore because my body wouldn't let me stand around like a cow. I bought a pair of white tennis shoes because they gave me even more bounce and quickness, and Nick didn't like those shoes one bit. Nor did it help that it hurt me to make love for months after the hospital. The frigid speed queen: they started calling me *Syl* instead of Sylvia right after I dyed my hair black, for the first time, and when I put off marrying Nick for probably the third time, he yelled at me that I had *become* scar tissue, and went off to the east coast with a bimbo named Jeanette.

"So there you have it up to stage two in the transmogrification of Sylvia Winnoe, *née* Boyd. And you know the rest, Mungo, you know I'm no butterfish this time around. But when the cops took Bip and me into the Women's House of Detention this morning, I thought, my God, what can I become next? Some sort of cucumber with a parrot voice and no sex organs whatsoever?

"I was pretty sure they wouldn't hold us long with you in town, but the minute I was run into the elevator up to the tank, with all these little college girls with trembling upper lips who were still shouting *pig* and other things guaranteed to provoke the matrons, and even though Bip was right there holding on to me, I still thought I was doomed to go through it all again, and come out for the third time — hospital, Terminal Island, House of Detention — even smaller! Still, it was funny when Bip and I came back down the elevator after the matron said we made bail, funny because we knew only one bailmaker in all of Manhattan. What relief to see you in the hallway . . . I mean, you looked like the fanciest uptown lawyer in the book. Pin-striped suit! Croquet, you're too much.

"And now you're hopped on the silly idea that Stanley may be an informer, a police spy in California drag. Not that I believe you — you're not always right, you geek — that he could have had something to do with the bust this morning. No, we were just in the wrong place at the wrong time. But there *is* something scary about the coke wilderness Stanley lives in. Dammit, though, I like the man, Bip loves him to death, and I flat don't understand why he hasn't been to see her, if he really is in New York like you say.

"Like you say; you say nothing. You want me to pull away your layers one by one, like an artichoke — ha ha — until I come to the heart, which will be what? A pale little boy thumbing his nose at the whole fucking world. I know,

I talk too much; I should just help you with your little bombers and be done with it; just ball you some more and be done with it; just find Nick and be done with it; just leave all of it and see if I can survive on my lonesome.

"What would happen if I pulled off this mustache of yours? Will there be another underneath? And whose hair is this anyway? See! Look at you pull away. You've got all these control strings running out to people, you've got a piano wire to my crotch right now, but you won't let me pull myself toward you. What are you afraid of, Mungo, huh? If you were stripped down to the *nut,* would you simply grow smaller and smaller before my eyes? Or would I only find a zephyr of hot gas at the core?

"I don't care; when we make love it's like the beginning of the universe.

"Maybe you think you're some sort of urban Pan — an electric Faun who can run freely through this dumb civilization . . . with spiky black bombs for balls, and a silver cock instead of a cross. Oh dear, I didn't mean to offend him, this ruby knight in your frosted bush. I remember when you came out of the sea in Mexico. Out of the Pacific in Manzanillo, and my new-husband Nicholas Winnoe, genuinely startled, amazed out-of-character, said, 'For the love of God, will you look at that person!'

"I could see you reflected in Nick's mirror-sunglasses, see how *white* you were even on the exaggerating silver nitrate of the lenses — a pillar of salt rising from the navy sea. It was extraordinary. I bet Nick still believes you'd never gone into the water in the first place, that you emerged fullblown from a volcanic fissure, like Aquaman.

"And when you came over you seemed to straddle us. You're not that tall, but there you were, and I could see Nick struggling to conceal his attraction to you. Then you said whatever it was, a smuggler's come-on that was bound to impress the tough ex-college students. Don't tell me. It was, 'Have you folks tried the *camarones* or the *ceviche* from the *palapa* down the beach?' Each Spanish word lingered over with your goddamn ironic drawl. Yes, Señor Croquet, El

Supremo, was always persuading us to try something *further* on down the beach . . . and now I think maybe you're going too far.

"No! Don't get up, I'm sorry, I didn't mean it. A joke.

"I don't want to be serious, but when you make some pontification like, say, Henry Kissinger is a Rasputin, or a high-priest to an antiChrist, I think you forget that he isn't much taller than I am and looks like a cartoon in person. His nose pores are like raspberry seeds, and he uses a lilac talc on the back of his neck. He's a person, Mungo. A human being. I don't want to be serious, to think of evil drifting down like the soot outside your window there; I want to go lie in the country-grass and feel the sun for a change.

"Oh damn you, touch me like that again and I'll crap."

Croquet said, "You have the beautiful habit of making a farrago of the absurd things people like me say," and he then touched her again on the perfect scar, the pads of his fingers making an excruciating commentary along its length, until soon he was stretched alongside her, and she could close her eyes but still retain the ghostglow of him in the apartment's quickening afternoon light. In her mind he disappeared and was replaced by indigo ponds that she had risen above, and while she began to soar over them he kissed lightly the hollow of her throat and the way down to the nodes of her breasts. One of his hands had come up to cup her groin, the center-pressure growing until she was penetrated *that is exactly right* just enough to be able to maintain her equilibrium, as below her the ponds skipped and shimmered and threw up reflections of her body as it sailed like a transparent scrim in the blue breeze.

For her, the outside alarums of traffic became geese, crows, white drakes on the ponds; she turned into him, offering more of herself to his hand, his mouth, insisting that his lapping of her breasts reveal the kite-string connection between nipples and clitoris and the bottom cervix of her, where his pressure had not got. She reached blindly for the grave curve of his buttock, let her own fingers slide down the fresh cool soil of his skin until they might brush the rim of his anus *goodness* and braille the down of his balls. His hand left off inside her, his legs scissored, and as his mouth rose to hers, came keenly into hers, she slid her hand the perimeter of his thigh so that it rested on the taut presence of his cock which she now handled into herself almost roughly *oh*. Why was her tongue never long enough to flay the roof of his mouth? She forced her pelvis forward, (plummeting out of the sky), with both hands on his rear, until *there* it was all the way into her, and his ribcage pressed against the fiery scar.

Momentarily, she rolled him on his back *more now* and could lower her still-blind head to one of his nipples and suck so hard she was afraid, could almost feel the blood rising up through his pale flesh and into her mouth. His hands nipped her waist, kept her steady on, bouncing, while she welted and spittled his chest. She heard herself growling; it was a darkness in her head *what is he saying?* with pin-splashes of light off in the distance, one pink flash of pain as his finger found and briefly entered her anus . . . then went on to press his cock forward and up *please* and she had to find a place on his neck where the tendon was heated and throbbing, a place to fix upon, to cleave her lips to, while she beat her body up and out of this darkness and into the illuminated air again *Mungo!*

The bones of her toes must soon crack. She raised from him. Slapping. He was hitting her breasts lightly from side to side *no, no, can't he hear me?* He did. They were over, flipped, still. She took his ass and directed it to do slowly what she wanted. Now, the almost mechanical kissing, just something there, wet, while the pressure grew inside her. So still though *perfect:* it's out there somewhere. She saw it, went for it, growing rigid *let him, now,* and there and there, all gone all gone. He was battering her now, but it didn't matter   because she was snapped, roiling and done.

While he stiffened above her she kept to herself the still

laughter within her; his torso arched up and away and he rent the air with the weird cry of semen lost to her. But then she was released to laughter. She could see the ponds again, could open her eyes to the long corpse of him . . . to the golden haze of the room, to the disinterested fish in the tank that looked down upon the bed. She laughed, wondering what were words compared to this? And laughed again, until he raised his moon face and she said, "The Big Bang theory is correct."

He rolled off, gradually, he just easily slipped right out of her, and she groaned. But then was happy to stretch, to flex, to know the airy wetness of her own unstoppered insides.

Now he was flat on his back, preoccupied as usual, cold and alabaster against the sheets, his penis wilted and raw amid the perspiring icicles of his pubic hair.

"Mungo, what happens now?" She touched him. He raised an eyebrow — dyed? — over an eye as blue as her sky ponds.

"You could call your husband," he said lazily. "You could go see Bip at Perry Street. You could help me find that scalawag Stanley. You could wish the police hadn't finger-printed you this morning. You could feed the fish. You could stand in the window and be seen by my neighbor Leonard the Groper. Or you could go uptown to the library and brush up on your Fanon, your Cleaver, or even your old Camus."

As he merrily drew out the last syllable she tweaked him gently and said, "I'll call Nick, then go see Bip."

"Suit yourself, my friend," he said. "We can all meet later at the Riviera. The impresario Decatur Samson is in town, and I have an idea he might know how to find Stanley. Wouldn't you like to have dinner with old Decatur?"

"Yes sir. He's such a charming fellow."

He palmed her vulva and they got up into the world again.

Sylvia picked up Croquet's telephone and dialed the numbers he had given her before he left the apartment rigged out in the corduroys, the desert boots and the immaculately hung auburn hair. Goodbye, pin stripe suit. She waited for the circuits to connect. Nick. She felt, standing nude just a few steps from the open window, the traffic blaring sixty feet below her, a sense of nervous playfulness that only increased as the fuzzed rings of the other telephone sounded in her ear. Come on, Nick; be waiting there for me for once in your life, you penguin, you hairy cuckold. She was ready to forgive him for the two years of silence; hell, she hadn't written *him* either. Did it all come down to dumb stubbornness? But now, she'd had Croquet. Nick could have the forgiveness. Fair trade. She even grinned slyly at this generosity on the part of the person she knew to be a willful adultress.

" 'Lo." A girl's voice.

Sylvia was too disappointed to be polite. "Who's this?" she demanded. In the silence she thought she could hear a child wailing.

"It's Monica Baldi. Do you want Pablo?"

"I want Nick Winnoe."

"Oh sure, just a minute I'll get him."

Her anxiety expanded like crystals within her and she didn't know why. She pinched the tight flesh of her thigh, as a reminder that she was no supplicant, that no one's permission was being asked for anything, that she was just as free as the man to whom she was about to talk. But she knew the problem was that she was nowhere near as free as, say, the provider of these seamy Manhattan orgasms. The guilt was stabilizing, and gave pain.

Over the phone came the sounds of male yelling, of disjointed cries heard — it seemed — through the medium of water. A man's voice shouted "Sara!" and even the remote transmission could not modulate the twang of anger in his voice. There was the squealing and thumping of children, and the voice began again, "Sara, we're going now." Then the other phone seemed to be striking against a wall with amplified force. *Thunk thunk.*

54

"Is somebody there?" the voice said. "Is someone there?"

"I'd like Nick, please," she replied, and was quite taken aback by the response.

"Nick! Good fucking Christ! What sort of *zoo* is this? For all I know he's cornholing a duck."

Before Sylvia could speak, the phone banged against the wall again and a high-pitched yowling commenced in the background. It probably *was* a menagerie — Nick's newest, complete with lachrymose children and at least one sorely wounded adult.

"Hello." Now here was the voice she wanted; the syllables came smoothly, naturally.

"Nick," she said, trying to put into the word all the blessings she hoped for.

"Uh-oh." His unstudied reaction did bring her a certain pleasure; she smiled at one of the groupers in Croquet's motley fishtank. "Syl," Nick said, "hold on . . . " and at a distance, as if through layers of suet, she could hear him saying, "Lucia, it's my wife, can you keep these kids quiet . . . Little uproar here, Syl."

"How are you, Nick?"

"I'm fine, I'm good. You all right?"

Indeed, she was. "Yes," she said.

"Look, let's not talk now. I can call you later. At Wicket's?"

Would she be put off so easily?

"Yes," she said.

"*Adiós, chula,*" he said, forcefully.

So much for that. She replaced the phone in its bed, looking out of the window as she did so, and saw across the way, in the window of a crummier building, a tiny man in a Hawaiian shirt who was giving her the hairy eyeball. This — it must be Leonard the Groper — cheered her; no more had she wanted, and so she waved gayly at Leonard, but he didn't move. Sylvia turned about and offered him a view of her rear end, then walked the length of the room to try and coax a shower from Croquet's coffin-sized stall.

Afterwards, she had the simple problem of clothes for a

Friday night in the city: Mungo, Bip, Decatur, and Sylvia modestly on the town; or searching out one red-headed screwball. Whichever, she couldn't wear the dress Bip had made her buy at the airport, with its detention grime, and perhaps — yes — linked splotches of puke from that girl who had had her stomach whispered over with the nightstick of the cop this morning. No, this thing wouldn't do. She went to Croquet's closet and found, lo and behold, a tidy nest of items of female apparel, from which she selected a flowered, wrap-around frock of thin muslin. Over her bare shoulders she hung a tan suede jacket, also from the closet; in its pockets she found balled kleenex and some change. She took an extra set of keys to Croquet's and left the apartment for 18 Perry Street, where Bip would be waiting.

Through a lovely twilight she went, pleased to be out and moving, nagged only by the thought that Bip might not have connected with Stanley. And, yes, when Bip answered the ornate doors of the townhouse, her proud face was scrunched into petulance.

"Where've you been, sister? They've got me doing nigger work in here. I fly all the way across the United States of America, I get hassled and rousted and busted, and then when I think there's a chance to catch my breath and figure out what's going on with my Stanley, you jilt me for an illicit afternoon in bed, right?, while *I* get relegated to cleanin' up the lavish kitchen of these birdbrain revolutionaries . . . Come on, kiss me and I'll be all right."

Sylvia happily kissed her lips and they went inside, to the lighted kitchen where pots, pans, dishes, glassware stood drying on the sideboard, and half of the floor had been scrubbed to a gleam, while the remainder stood dull with grit and scuffings.

"You look real good," Bip went on, peering askance at her own grubby shift. "I want to finish up and take a shower and get something decent to eat."

"No Stanley, huh?" Sylvia asked.

Bip glared. "No. I'm beginning to think Croquet made it all up about seeing him. There's nobody here but these pipsqueaks."

"Really?" Now that she was here, Sylvia's curiosity began to work on what before had been only a wooly obtuseness in Croquet's general rhetoric.

"You bet," Bip said. "That Sammy is upstairs. There's another man down in the basement, and the girl Elaine is somewhere around, too."

"What the hell is this?"

"I do *not* know," Bip replied. "I do know that Elaine's momma and poppa own this place, and that they're returning from Barbados just exactly tomorrow, and I don't reckon they would want to find any dangerous substances on the floor or anything like that. So yours truly is setting the place right . . . at Mr. Croquet/Silver/Wicket's request, of course."

"Take it easy, Bip," Sylvia said gently. "We'll finish this and get out of here. Go to dinner. Get high. Okay?"

"Well, I've done my part and I'm gonna take me a shower. You do the rest."

Bip lifted her shift over her head and dropped it on the unclean portion of the kitchen floor.

"I just might take what's left of the money and fly straight back to California, you know," she said, and turned and walked flat-footed and oaken into the bathroom. Sylvia took a step after her, wishing like the devil to speak something soothing and reasonable, but the harsh sound of the water jet striking the metal shower stall made the wish seem futile, and instead she turned her attention to the kitchen proper and how best to finish the job of work Bip had begun. She took off the jacket and hung it on one of the chairs.

The bucket that sat on the floor in front of the sink she filled with hot water, added more soap, and stirred with the fat sponge that Bip had been using. Carefully hitching up the muslin skirt she kneeled down by the table and began to scrub the blemished linoleum in widening circles.

The sound, when it came, deafened her immediately: so that even though the first explosive concussion knocked her on her side, one hip in the filmy puddle of water; and though most of the kitchen floor seemed to disappear with the second blast, leaving her on a jagged island of linoleum; and though the fine talcum-like rain of plaster and brick dust had magically fogged the air everywhere about her . . . even so, she was able to say, to herself, "Oh boy, I'll never be able to clean this up," while she dumbly continued to scrub, as it were, the milky air, but now squeezing the sponge so tightly that clots of water flew from her circling hands.

Her comprehension of the absurdity of what she was doing arrived soon enough, and later she would recall how precisely she conceived of and ordered her actions once she had determined that in the midst of the terrible chaos of particles and smells she had no injury other than the shrill ringing — more like whispered *crashing* — in her ears.

As she flung away the sponge her brain ticked off curt items: there's going to be a fire; get Bip; the lights are still on; out out out. She went on her knees, edging and slipping to reach the jacket trapped beneath the fallen chair; then she was upright and picking her way around a jagged wound of torn floor ligaments, and the lights began to flicker. Past the queerly slumped refrigerator until she could make out the bathroom door, which was still closed, intact, even though parts of the surrounding walls had been blown clear through, and Sylvia could see beyond the shards of plaster that still clung to the wall studs that the bathroom space was at least *there* . . . even that it was relatively free of acrid dust, almost normal-looking. But the damn door wouldn't budge for her. "Bip!" She yanked and kicked and finally had the sense to reach an arm through one of the holes and fumble for the bolt. In. She ripped back the shower curtain and found Bip perfectly rigid, a fist pressed against either wall of the stall. She stared at Sylvia with a mix of fright and accusation, as if Sylvia herself had blown the place to smithereens. Sylvia slapped her. "Come on, idiot!" And Bip stumbled forth, all trembling gooseflesh and so much a zombie that Sylvia had no choice but to hurl the jacket over her shoulder, jerk the lapels across her breasts, gripping the bunches of leather in one fist, and lead Bip like a dray horse back into the kitchen.

Half-way across the room the lights finally died. "Goddammit!" Sylvia screamed, sure they would fall through one fissure or another, into the basement, but she was driven forward by her fear of the fire that she believed she could smell even then, like smoldering cotton batting or scorched wool. As she moved blindly through the murk with her numb charge, the dull pressure in her nostrils increased and she thought *gas* at the same time she became convinced the ceiling was about to dump itself right upon them. But, finally, they were in the hallway; she turned them left and used her free hand to discover the length of the wall and then the fat cool door knob. As soon as she had the doors open on the still dusk of Perry Street, she knew worse matters were in store. "Oh Jesus, people," she moaned. A man was pointing at her; two or three others backed away along the sidewalk on the other side of the street.

Sylvia had Bip half-way down the stoop before she remembered her friend's near-nakedness. Knowing very well that such a thing was irrelevant, Sylvia looked back. She saw that Bip was covered by the jacket, at least to her crotch; and she saw, too, down the haze of the long hallway above them, a figure staggering toward the light of the street. And just as she unloosed the lapels of Bip's jacket in order to go help the person, the hallway disappeared with a sigh, a shudder; a whoosh of pulverized stuff flew into her face and over Bip's hair with almost no noise whatsoever. Everything stopped dead, frozen. Sylvia seemed to have one leg suspended in the air . . . when someone yelled from a great distance, "Get away from there! Get away!"

Yes. She turned and wrapped an arm around Bip's shoulders; she used her other hand to hold the jacket shut, and embracing her friend tightly she directed them the rest of the way to the sidewalk, and they went on up Perry Street, like lovers strolling, you would have thought.

Sylvia heard a voice.

"Here, girls, come in here."

A woman, several houses away, stood at the top of her stoop; she was peering down at them, clearly frightened, but motioning to them. This must be a haven. Up. Quickly. The

woman was middle-aged, sleek; she bowed them across her
threshold, but in her agitation clutched and fumbled at the
beads around her neck. "What is it? What is it?" she repeat-
ed. "Is the gas main gone and exploded? Look at you both!
My husband told me they were sixty or seventy years old. Do
you know?"

Sylvia couldn't seem to catch her breath for speech. Bip
had slumped against the wall of the foyer. Her jacket gaped.

"Do I know what?" Sylvia managed to expell.

"How old the gas mains are?" Sylvia stared at the
woman's vermillion mouth, and realized that the third ex-
plosion had probably been just that, the old gas main, deep
down, that would collapse the floors, and the goddamn hall-
way. The woman chattered on. "I mean, the rats surely gnaw
them. Don't you think so?" Sylvia nodded, thinking must
retrench, regroup, this is unreal. "Wouldn't you like to lie
down? And you could have a bath . . . that's it!" The lady
was overjoyed. "You both must have a bath. It's so dirty
here in Manhattan."

Bip was nodding like a junkie against the wall. Her body
was so lax that Sylvia thought she might fall into a dark, hope-
less heap on the floor; she moved quickly to prevent it. She
wanted them to be alone, yes, and maybe she could bring Bip
out of her shock, or whatever it was. Somewhere in the dis-
tance the sirens began to *whoop*, zeroing in on this neighbor-
hood, this block. "Yes, please," Sylvia said, "maybe we could
clean up."

"Wonderful, wonderful, come this way. This certainly
will be a surprise for your father, the poor man."

"What?" Sylvia abruptly stopped her effort to shove
and prod Bip up the stairs behind their hostess. "What did
you say?"

The woman looked down at her in a kindly manner.
"Well, aren't you Elaine Freeman? You must be. Before
your father went off to the islands he told me you would be
in the house writing a book on politics. Isn't that right?"

"Uhh . . . " In her mind's eye she saw a female corpse
riddled with roofing nails — she didn't know why. "Yes.

Something like that, yeah."

The woman nodded smugly, and they continued on up the stairs and into what must have been her bedroom. The furniture was down-stuffed and very white. Bip could stand alone now, her muscles were functioning again. But Sylvia could see no signs of comprehension in her gleam-less eyes.

From the bathroom the woman called out, "I'll run a tub," and the water splashed. The *whoop whoop* of the sirens grew louder, and Sylvia's chest felt as if it were running from the rest of her body: she could not visualize any way out of this; no money, no Croquet . . . both of them jailbirds, one of them catatonic.

Still the chattering went on, as the woman returned, " . . . so when you and your friend are tidy we'll call a doctor and talk to the police and I hope—" Suddenly her face twisted into a parody of terrible concern. "Oh goodness, there was nobody else in your house was there?"

Sylvia shook her head, trying to keep her lips from trembling.

"I'm so glad. Pheww. Here's a bathrobe for your friend. I'll be downstairs." And she was gone at last.

"Bip!" Sylvia hissed.

Downstairs in the street the sirens moaned and faded.

Something began to happen in Bip's eyes. Fluid shone, tears, and they stared at one another for the first time in what seemed to Sylvia to be years and years. She went close to Bip and sensed that her trembling was barely controlled. Bip lifted both arms from beneath the jacket and embraced Sylvia's neck. Their foreheads met as Bip whispered, "There's three people dead in that house, little sister."

Again Sylvia saw the torso studded with bits of bright metal. She put her arms around Bip and squeezed; she pressed herself against the larger woman until their mutual tremors were for the moment cancelled. "What are we going to do, Bip-O?"

"Go." She came near to pressing the breath out of Sylvia. "Get some clothes and leave on out of here."

"Just go?" Sylvia was losing her way; she staggered back

and almost fell onto the opulent bed.

"Yes, open that closet."

Sylvia did so, glad to do what she was told, but the closet was too full for decisions. She stood gaping at the linens and silks.

"That raincoat, trenchcoat, whatycallit, give me that," Bip said. Sylvia stripped the pink material — it was a cape — from its hanger and handed it over. Bip engulfed herself in it, and now she looked almost debonair except for the layer of chalky dust that covered her face and webbed her hair.

"We're covered with crap," Sylvia wailed.

"Lord! In the bathroom, quick, rub some of it off, then git."

They moved, fast. Wash cloth, towel, anything would do. Sylvia managed the jacket over her soiled muslin dress and they were ready. She followed Bip to the head of the stairs where they waited until they were sure the owner of the house was not in evidence, that she was probably out in the street because the front door was still open. Down they went. Human shouts came through the door from the street, shouts mixed with loud and frantic *hissing.* In the doorway they halted. Bip peeked around the edge of the entryway while Sylvia pressed against her back. "Oh oh oh," Bip breathed, and Sylvia craned to see over her shoulder; saw the confusion of fire engines and squad cars, saw smoke, saw arcs of silver water shooting into the wreck, saw clumps of people all pressed together behind the police sawhorses. Oh, to be back in the joint again, she thought, and gripped Bip's cape as if it were a stuff that would make her invisible — oh, to be covered with flesh, to be passive and jolly and safe. But it was now, and Bip was breathing beneath the cape like a willful animal, and Sylvia knew they would move.

They descended the stairs and by silent agreement assumed an attitude of calm purposefulness. They turned right. And walked, you could see, straight on up Perry Street, away from the fractured townhouse.

CHAPTER FIVE

I heard the sound of a clown who cried in the alley.

New England
May 1, 1970

YOU could see, too, the Blount sedan spin out of the Eaton
driveway in the purples and greens of dusk. Blount was in-
tensely aware that as he drove the grey road home with a
feigned casualness, Sara sat beside him implacable and wind-
blown.

When Blount had walked away from Pablo Eaton in the
cemetery he had felt himself to be properly adjusted, emotion-
ally aligned with a knowledge about Sara that he never for a
moment doubted. His cool lasted him up the hill to the house
and enabled him to stand near the ashy hibachi with the others,
and even to savage a piece of red meat stuck between rolls and
onion.

But when the sound of the telephone had summoned
Monica — *his wife's lover* — to the innards of the house; when
Pablo's scrofulous dog had appeared near the duck pond with
a sizeable rock in his chops; and when Lucia Eaton had said,
"Pablo's on a diet of gin and eggs," Blount's delicate tolerance

collapsed.

His shout had made them all jump. Before his sons could flee, he had seized their wrists and sent towards Sara sufficient silent disgust to inform her they would be leaving directly. But she merely stared, in surprise, and so he took the boys through the backdoor as if they were his personal baggage, which they demonstrated they were not by slipping from his grip in the hallway of photographed mummies, where Blount collided with Monica, solidly. She smiled, or had she smirked? He had passed on down the hall with such an inchoate oath that his children in front of him began to scuttle in fear. He caught up with them in the mossy kitchen where Oliver was pointing at the telephone left suspended and swinging from its wall-cradle. "We're going now," he called out, and grabbing the telephone he found himself shouting nonsense that now, in his own automobile, on his way to his own house, he could hardly remember.

Instead, his fickle memory provided one succinct fact: he had forgotten his goddamn bicycle. He forced himself to say calmly, almost apologetically, "I left my bike," although he knew that Sara, whose hand rested casually on his knee as if to soften the rage she could surely sense in his rigid driving movements, would take his remark 'as an opportunity to bait him, where earlier she might have wished to placate.

"Did you, love?" she asked.

Oliver's head appeared in the rearview mirror. "Daddy, I know where your bike is."

He attempted playfulness. "Where?" It hurt.

"In the barn. Nick put it there, I saw him."

"You mean he took it out of his truck?" Wouldn't they leave him alone?

Oliver frowned. "Sure, how else—"

"Daddy," Sara interrupted, speaking plainly, without the usual lilt-for-children in her voice, "knows perfectly well how the bicycle got into the barn, and why it's going to stay there until tomorrow morning when he will go and get it." She put pressure on his knee, in punctuation.

"I will not!"

"Chris . . . what is the *matter* with you? You've been behaving like a fool ever since you got up this morning. Do you have a hangover? Maybe it's a concussion from dumping off your bike."

He snorted. "Do you know who it was who ran me off the road, do you?" Sara gazed ahead through the windshield. "That porcine Winnoe, that's who."

Now she was patting him, and laughing gently, so gently he wanted to scream. "Come on," she said, "Nick told me it was an accident . . . just a weird confluence."

Blount winced. *"Weird confluence?"*

"Just shut your hole for a while, love," she said in a friendly way, and while the boys in the rear giggled like demented things at her imperative, she leaned over and whispered lewdly in his ear, "I've got a surprise for you after the kids are in bed."

"No," Blount groaned. And they came home.

While Sara arranged the children upstairs, Blount remained foursquare in the kitchen. Ritual compelled him to take a stainless steel ice bucket from a shelf and place it on the counter near the door to the porch. From the cabinet below he brought up a half-gallon of bourbon, another of gin, another of rum; these he put beside the ice bucket. In the refrigerator he found a bottle of tonic, and a plastic tray of ice from the freezer compartment. The staples were assembled. No, he'd forgotten the lime, which he found gleaming in one of the vegetable drawers. The numb safety of things. He twisted the tray so that the ice cracked and clunked into the bucket; he replaced the lid; he re-watered the tray and put it in its proper place; he cut the lime into exact quarters and arranged them on a bonewhite plate. Things. Tasks. Repeated patterns. Rigid *methods.* But they didn't hold, wouldn't suffice: he seized a stemmed wineglass, hefted the bourbon, filled the glass, and swallowed down the liquid like medicine, a plash of cold heat among the meat, bread and onion in his gut.

Now he found himself in front of the alcoved record player. The galleys of THINGS BURST lay curling atop the ancient sideboard to his right. Oh brother. He flipped the phonograph's reject button, willing to accept whatever happened to be on the turntable at the moment, but he was hardput to tolerate the thin pop-voice that came wailing into the room as Tom and Oliver's bath shrieks struck his consciousness.

Blount worked his nose with the ball of one thumb and then lowered the volume on the infernal noise, thinking *pap.* His eyes swung idly to the top galley page, the same that Sara had been reading when he returned from his bicycler's brush with mortality. A shadow passed through his brain. The whiskey? He shook his head, but the pattern of words and white space on the galley page seemed to fall into meaningless hieroglyphics no matter how he altered the focusing of his eyes; the very spaces between the words conspired to form a cartoon figure — a male with a grossly swollen member pointing toward the upper left corner of the page. As quickly as he saw the illusion it disappeared, the words returned to words, and Blount read, to his horror, the sentence: *"Oh, don't you know the regina is the dirtiest . . . "* He took a deep breath, whispered the reassuring word, *paranoia,* and found a pen with which he carefully noted the typographical error, writing out the correction in the margin: *vagina.*

Christ, he was tired, and thus when his children came down to him shining brownly in the living room's dim light, he self-consciously gathered them in his arms and carried them to the couch, where they could sit as a kind of enclave against the coming of their mother who was still at her duties above.

Tom sat stolidly in the crook of his elbow, but Oliver, on the other side and no longer accustomed to the closeness of Blount's thick body, fidgeted and finally twisted from his grasp, saying, "Dad, Mommy said you'd tell us a story, a real one with a good ending."

Blount all of a sudden felt fat with tears that had better not come now. "Did she?"

"Ngggh," Tom said. Blount hugged him so hard the thumb popped from his mouth and he smiled, quite beautifully.

"Once upon a time," Blount began, "there was a plant named Rufus Pebo Weaver."

Oliver's eyes registered amazement. "What?"

"A green plant, okay?" Oliver relaxed. "Rufus took so many vitamins that he grew tremendously tall, so tall that he fell over, his roots pulled up, and he died. The end."

"Ahhh," Oliver wailed, "that story's too short."

"Chris, that's a really good story," Sara said from the balcony railing. Blount craned his head and saw that she was smiling down on them from the shadows. What sort of mawkishness is burrowing here? he wondered, at the same time thinking that she looked like a willowy idol . . . *benevolent, wise and fair.*

Sara moved along the balcony on her way to the stairs; he could see her hand, attenuated, skeletal, trail along the rail top as she went.

I will not have it! his brain shouted. She is *not* about to get away from me. No!

When the children had left him, with solemn handshakes all round, Blount climbed from the relative safety of the couch and after switching on a lamp or two followed Sara into the kitchen for the remainder of their drink ritual . . . and on this evening he could no more predict the outcome than he could know whether Sara would drink rum, gin or bourbon. He stood and watched her as she bent into the refrigerator to affirm her perfect knowledge of its contents; he watched the cotton of her dress tighten over her ass as she bent further, peering. The material rose away from her back thighs and he wanted to run his fingertips the whole length of her legs.

"You're not hungry, are you," she said, telling him that he shouldn't be, that nothing would get *fixed* on this evening. She unbent, shut the door, and turned to him with the tip of her middle finger just leaving her tongue with a soft kissing sound. "Are you?"

"What?" he said, his head full of Monica suddenly. "Oh, no. Would you like a drink?"

Her eyes stared into space, out to that place where she consulted her private tastes. "I'd like a glass of chilled white wine," she enunciated.

A blast of inner heat made shards of his wit, of his imagined control over the situation. He felt drunk and useless and the phonograph singing bleated into his ears.

She was moving toward him. "Are you going to faint?" she asked. One of her hands stretched out and came to rest like wax on his shoulder.

He had to move out of her range; the hand dropped away and he said, "No, not at all. I'll just get the wine, I'll just get it for you." He passed safely by her, reached into the refrigerator and found the pale chilly bottle in his hand, and as he turned to locate a glass he discovered that she held beneath his nose the same glass that had contained his toot of bourbon. He said nothing, though, believing even as he poured the wine that she would see the syrupy glaze of the earlier liquid. If she did, she didn't care, and, the glass being full, she walked away from him into the living room, as the record finally ended with the muted shifts and clicks of the mechanism turning itself off.

Quiet. He poured himself a tumbler of the same wine and went to join his wife. She had arranged herself at one end of the long maple table they kept in front of an expanse of glass that looked out on their backyard, garden, and the dark plowed fields and mashed hills beyond. The outer twilight was cut into squares, now, by the cracked and greying mullions that neatly framed Sara's head, which he saw shot about with cigarette smoke: the lamp-lit golden aura of her; and above her, over the fireplace, the large and languid nude — an oil that someone had given her long ago.

Blount sat himself in an armchair at the opposite end of the table. While Sara slouched in her own chair, the cigarette held near her head in two benedicting fingers, Blount sat with his back stiff, his elbows resting on the chair arms, his hands loosely intersected between his spread legs. Protecting himself, you might have thought.

They sipped. She smoked. After a moment, he began to smoke. He fetched another ash tray, resumed his position, and knew — soberly — that if he but looked at her, the "surprise" she had mentioned earlier would be delivered with all the panache she could muster, or so he believed whenever he sniffed the delicate fumes of the wine they were drinking. If what she was going to say had anything to do with Monica and what Pablo Eaton had told him in the cemetery, then he would probably break her back. He looked down at his hands, at the ridiculous cigarette that blemished them, and knew that he *could* . . . over his knees, like a piece of kindling.

"Well," she said, "I'm having this love affair with Monica."

Out of his control his left foot began to jiggle, and he supposed that he was frowning and tried to correct it; he hadn't quite looked at her yet; now he wished he had broken Pablo Eaton's back instead. When he did finally bring his head up for a composed gaze — and not without raising a hand at the same time, a hand that mashed his nose almost flat against the plane of his face — he discovered that Sara was regarding him quite openly, matter-of-factly; indeed, she might have just said, 'I'm having some photographs made of Monica.' But she had not.

"Really?" he said. He found that his voice zinged and wavered in the air like Oliver's. "Why are you doing that?"

"Will you listen if I tell you?"

"What's that supposed to mean?" Careful.

"Sometimes you only listen to the beginning," she said evenly. "Then you turn off, go away . . . you absent yourself."

"Me?" Her exaggerated eloquence had given him a fright. Was she teasing him? "I'll stay here," he said, careful to insert an edge of ruefulness in his tone.

"See! Already you're being cute."

"Sara, I'm listening."

Her eyes were in the distance again. "It's very good with her, that's all. I was afraid, but now I know I can handle it."

Blount didn't know whether he was hearing a simple, sensual description, or some kind of lonely double-dare. If he asked what she meant, would she subject him to some delicate version of her experiences with Monica? Or would she leap to her feet, hurl the glass at his face, and cry, 'What are you going to do about it?' He was in a quandry; a sexual thicket into which jealous lust for his wife came creeping like a sloth.

"What are you thinking?" she asked quietly.

"I'm wondering what it's like." He seemed to have chosen to be objective, or fair-minded, although he was not aware of choosing anything.

"You bastard, you lying son-of-a-bitch," she said easily, laughing at the same time, the laughter cradling the words in the air between them.

"You know very well," he said, "you can do what you please."

"As long as I keep my lesbian self separate from being a mother, a cook, a lover to you?"

He hesitated. What words had he written that morning? *I have to discover my lesbian self.* Was his half-assed fiction now predicting his life? He thought of the obscene hieroglyphics of his proofs and shuddered . . . though he kept Sara from seeing that he had. You've got to lie to them, always; and he answered his question: "Yes, why not?"

"You'll *share* me?"

He bit off the word "Yes," and watched her stand and slowly circle the couch, her arms hugged beneath her breasts. She looked preoccupied, almost sullen, as if she were trying to master a new, many-faceted domestic problem. He gnawed at the flesh around the nail of his middle-finger, right hand.

Finally, she came near to him and ruffled his hair in a way that was both affectionate and harsh; her knuckles rapped his scalp briefly, and he didn't look up at her when she said, "Monica is a kind person." Whether the noise he then made was a groan or a grunt or a mumble of agreement, he knew she would never know, for she continued speaking as if he had made no sound at all. "She knows how hard a woman has to work at being an *individual;* she knows that words are as important as orgasms, that words can be as sublime as a licking tongue."

Now came the rushing impulse to rend this monstrous experience from his wife. No more the sloth. He was on his feet, near-crouched before her, his instant erection mocking his jock strap and cycling shorts. He swept his right hand in a wide circle, up to the feathery back of her neck, and forced her to bend toward him until her forehead touched his. With her head in his power he could make them circle, could lock her bright eyes to his as they revolved. But dammit, she was cooperating, and they too easily reached the rug in front of the couch, where, despite having to fend off her batting hands, he was able to reach low and clasp her behind the knee, to jerk once, upwards, shoving against her forehead at the same time, so that they both went down gracefully onto the thick animal shag.

He could see himself doing what he was doing. Sara's dress rolled and bunched over her midriff as his hand pawed her underwear to her knees, and then she did the rest as he pushed off his own lower garments. Anything quick would do: he must get a hand on himself and shove into the hairy kindness that she seemed to offer up to him, with a lasciviousness that would have frightened him had he not been so intent on entering where Monica could never reach. There! She gasped. He stopped — his cursed double-vision — to make sure that they agreed on the terms. And it was precisely the wrong thing to do. He had been mistaken. The tears lay on her cheeks like clear stones.

He withdrew, pulled out, rolled off. The rug tickled his face.

"Chris," she murmured.

"What?" he asked, between biting his forearm.

"Come to the bedroom."

Ahh, her terms. "What for?"

No answer.

When he heard her rise he turned his head to see her going away. Her back rippled at him and disappeared through the bedroom door. He noticed the grinding of his own teeth and rolled over, flung off the rest of his clothing, and went into the kitchen where, before turning out the light, he gulped down a dram of bourbon straight from the bottle.

But the liquid might as well have been water, so taut was he when he found his way into the bedroom where — *in candlelight; have mercy, Lorna Doone* — the woman was fixed belly-down in the exact center of the high bed, her burnished length a miracle of symmetry against the bas-relief wrinkles and whorls of the white sheets. Her ass was as still as death. He saw that she had placed a folded pillow beneath her hips, that this was why her buttocks curved at him like unnatural fruit. What was expected of him? The back of her head gave no clue; the candlelight was only a novelty.

He approached the edge of the bed, and when his penis touched the smooth wood of the high frame he had the good grace to realize that what he was being offered he must take; that if he didn't he would forever regret it. He must now make his body lie. Sara's reasons for demanding this thing didn't matter; he knew he had to perform. Drunken reasoning, perhaps, but his nonetheless.

If she speaks, he thought, I'll fucking leave; I'll take my typewriter and go right for the desert. But, of course, he was fretting for no one, and he soon saw that she knew well enough to keep mute, dream-silent, until his unsteady wit, his acquiescence, his penchant for calculation . . . all propelled him to the bathroom for a tiny dab of vaseline, a courtesy of sorts smeared on the candle-lit purple of his own grown penis.

Sara Leary Blount had won.

On Saturday morning before breakfast a befogged Blount was forced to take his sedan into Windsor for staples and a newspaper. He would not make use of Sara's electric blue 3-speed bicycle, nor would he make inquiries about his own, despite Sara's offer to drive him out to Eatons' to collect it. So he motored alone to the store, where in the narrow aisles he could jostle his neighbors for a chance at a pound of butter, two quarts of milk, a *New York Times,* and — on sour impulse — a half gallon tin of maple syrup, fresh from the tree, he hoped.

"You just bought some of Pablo Eaton's syrup." Nick Winnoe's hoarse tenor imparted this information over Blount's shoulder, causing him to twist around for a quick appraisal of this newest sally. He saw Nick's flaring nostrils, the gaping pores, a freshly shaved face that seemed dusted with talc; Nick was breathing loudly through his mouth, and as Blount moved away from him, once again the feeling struck that this pleasant hulk was physically kin to himself, although the other man was neither hungover nor skittish. Blount glanced at the syrup tin on the counter — "Bristol West Tree-Op," indeed — and then managed to tuck the tin in the sack with his other goods and move farther away from Nick, all in one dancing motion, he thought. But why did he find himself rocking back and forth on the curved-up toes of his cross-country shoes? Though Nick seemed to be paying no attention whatsoever, Blount felt as if he were somehow responding to silent instructions sent to him from Nick's unexplored brain. While Blount backed up the aisle in the direction of the door, Nick paid for a package of cigarettes and came on like a man intending to pass by with nary a word.

Blount had half-turned to precede him out of the store when he heard himself addressed again, directly. "What's bugging you anyway?"

Blount stopped. "Nothing at all, why do you ask?"

"You artless creep," Winnoe said with a smile. "I don't really think you're going to punch me out in front of the bologna. Let's go outside."

On the sidewalk, in the crisp morning sunlight, Blount faced his antagonist. Nick wore the same flapping and greasy jeans that he had worn to the picnic the day before, but today he had added an incongruously white jacket of a light material that hung like drapery over his rounded shoulders. Blount realized that because of the sun or the air his perceptions were clearing, and that today Nick didn't appear to be a man ready to banter about his mysterious wife or a babysitter's swell ass; instead, Blount noticed something canny and pinched about his eyes, about the set of his scraped jaw, which now seemed to have an unnatural blue tinge beneath the powdery whiteness . . . they stared at one another like wary brothers.

"Where do you live, Nick?" Blount asked, to pass the time of day and to shift the focus of attention away from himself. He felt the heaped events of the past twenty-four hours as an actual pressure at the back of his head as he stood waiting for Nick's response, but for now it seemed safe to chat, and if there was something wrong with Nick, well it needn't be Blount's problem.

"Just down there, over Marsh's garage." Nick pointed along the road with his pack of cigarettes, then tapped it on Blount's chest, pursing at the same time his thick lips. "Do you have any coffee at your house?"

"Sure."

"Don't you think a cup would do us both some good, help us handle this pissy world a little better, make us quits?"

"Quits?" Blount asked.

"You were rude to my wife Sylvia on the telephone yesterday."

Blount stared. "I was? I'm sorry, I didn't know who I was talking to."

"It's okay," Nick said. "I'll be up to your place later." He walked off in the direction of the garage, where Blount could see the cab of his pickup.

"Wait," Blount called. Winnoe turned. "Where's my bike?" Dumb question.

"I dunno," Winnoe said. "Aren't the roads safer with you separated from that machine?"

"My kid says you put it in Eaton's barn."

Nick smiled. "Then I guess I did. See you. Don't let that newspaper make you ill."

On his way home Blount shrugged off Nick's funny coy-
ness, and by the time he reached his own driveway he felt
clear-headed and reasonably content.

Oliver waylaid him as he stepped from the sedan.

"You have to play ball with me today, Daddy."

"Where's your mother?"

"In the garden. Tom got stung by a bee. What about—"

"He did?" Insect attacks frightened him. "Here, take
this stuff in the kitchen. Maybe we'll play this afternoon."

Blount went through the porch and into the backyard.
In the distance Sara bent to her garden's rows, attacking them
with a hoe. Short, hard chops with the blade. "Sara!"

She kept chopping as he approached. "What?"

"Where's Tom? Is he all right?"

"Sleeping . . . he was bee bit."

Blount's voice rose out of his control. "How do you
know he's not in a coma?"

Sara stopped her work and turned, the hoe shaft held
in her armpit and the crook of an elbow like a shotgun at rest;
she had turned with some exasperation, he realized. Sweat
glazed her forehead and caused her bangs to cling to it in
moist swatches. "Come again," she said.

"Did you put something on the sting?"

"Of course." She regarded him. "A little baking soda
and water." She hefted the tool, about to resume her work.
"I suppose you want breakfast."

"I'll get it. You sure he's all right?"

"Jesus, yes."

"Nick Winnoe's coming up for coffee," he said.

She had turned her back and begun to chop. "That's
nice . . . You can rant about . . . your . . . wives."

As Blount retreated he wondered if he could prepare
himself a batch of French toast as easily and as well as Sara
seemed to have taken control of her garden and her various
sexual selves. He thought he just might be able to. It was
Saturday morning, and once again the world was full of pos-
sibility: the ache in his genitals would disappear, as his
hangover already had; he would play catch with Oliver; the

75

visit from Winnoe might turn pleasant; and perhaps later, in the afternoon, he might return to his workroom and discover what it was he was trying to put on paper.

While he stood in the kitchen waiting for the toast to brown in the skillet, he unfolded the newspaper and cast an idle eye over the somber blacks and greys of the front page:

MITCHELL WARNS OF DANGER . . . NEW HAVEN POLICE SET OFF TEAR GAS AT PANTHER RALLY . . . ALLIES DRIVE AHEAD IN CAMBODIA; NIXON AGREES . . . CROWD OF YOUTHS HURL ROCKS . . . JOHNSON ASKS SUPPORT OF NIXON . . . U.S. ACTION LINKED . . . TOWNHOUSE EXPLOSION KILLS THREE . . . NIXON PUTS 'BUMS' LABELS ON SOME . . .

"You see these bums, you know, blowing up the campuses. Listen, the boys that are on the college campuses today are the luckiest people in the world, going to the greatest universities, and here they are burning up the books, storming around about this issue. You name it. Get rid of the war there will be another one."

Amused, as usual, by the combination of ignorance, absurdity, and hopelessness, Blount flipped his French toast, poured himself a glass of milk, and put some of Pablo Eaton's maple syrup in a sauce pan to heat. His eye then returned to the one story on the page which promised something immediate, something human, albeit violent:

Explosions and fire virtually demolished a townhouse at 18 Perry Street last night. Police have found three bodies, including the torso of a young woman riddled with roofing nails.

Some residents of the block reported seeing two young women flee the building shortly after the first blast, which splintered windows. Two more explosions followed, probably caused by ignited gas mains.

Police and firemen report finding a cache of dynamite in the same room with the torso of the young woman.

The townhouse belongs to Lionel Freeman, a Manhattan lawyer who is believed to be in Barbados.

Lawrence Nool, of 26 Perry Street., said that he had seen two women leaving the building. He described one as black and only partially clothed. "They just walked off," he said.

Firemen discovered 57 sticks of dynamite, 30 blasting caps, several yards of doorbell wire, 4 clock timers, and two fragmentation bombs.

Mercy, Blount said to himself, and when the phone began to ring — two shorts and a long for his household — the interruption was not unwelcome.

"Chris, this's Pablo Eaton."

What façade, what shield would do for this asshole? "Yes," he said sharply. There came to him a whiff of burnt toast. "Just a minute." He left the phone to take care of the skillet; his breakfast was now blackened and he returned to the telephone more than a little belligerent. "Now, what is it?"

"How you doin'?"

Blount snorted. "I'm okay, Pablo. How's yourself? And your daughter? Has she snuffed any ducks lately?"

"Hold the crud, Blount, I just wanted to tell you that Lucia found your bike in the barn."

"I know, I know," Blount said, irritation pulsing inside him like a headache; he couldn't figure out why he didn't simply shout at the other man. "Don't worry," he said, "I'll come and get it."

"No, no," Pablo spoke more rapidly, "I'll bring it to you; I've got to go to town this afternoon anyway."

"Well . . . shit, join the crowd."

"What?"

"I said thank you," he muttered, and heard Sara come into the kitchen behind him. "We'll be here all day."

"Later," Pablo said.

Blount hung up the phone and stood in the doorway looking at his grimy, lovely wife.

"Who that?" she asked.

"Eaton."

She looked surprised, then very nearly bitter. "Did you apologize to him?"

"What for? He's going to bring the bike."

"You bolted the party. You're the one who was rude . . . Oh, hell with it." She moved to butter the toast. "You put too much egg," she said with exasperation.

The simple criticism of his cooking did it. He didn't have to hold his tongue. "Sara, Pablo told me about you and Monica," he blurted. "Yesterday."

She dropped the knife on the counter and whipped around to face him. He'd gotten her; she had been robbed of her own revelation. "What! It's none of his business what I do!"

Despite himself, Blount smiled at her glint of rage, at the flash of honest snobbery; at least they shared this. Still, he could see her calculating his own portion of guilt in the conspiracy that had suddenly turned back on her; figuring the full meaning of his silence between the picnic and now.

But before she could voice anything, before she could identify and accuse his deception, there came an easy tapping on the frame of the porch door, and they both stared at Nick Winnoe, who said, "Knock, knock," hesitated a moment, sniffing the air, then came straight at them on his curiously stemmed legs; his thick torso bearing down gave Blount the feeling that a crude weight was being flung at him across the kitchen floor. Winnoe did not stop. He passed between Sara and Blount and into the living room, where he stalked a circle around the couch with quick looks for all of the objects of the room, particularly the pile of galleys on the sideboard.

"Something burns," he said, still moving.

With an exclamation Sara moved to the stove just as the syrup rose to a froth in the sauce pan. While she went about the motions of cleaning up, Blount poured two cups of coffee and took them and the newspaper into the living room, where Nick was now stopped near the table.

"Are you people alive?" he asked, taking the proffered cup. "Thank you. Or have I stepped into some waxworks?"

Blount put the paper on the table and watched Winnoe's eyes dart over the front page. He looked up.

"I see your galley proofs there, Chris; as a grease monkey I'm of course awed by the presence of such things, but don't think me some culture-fucking lout — a class rapidly oozing into these parts. I can be just as downhome and stupid as the next dirty-fingernailed person. Will you please say something, one of you, or I'll comment on that nude over the mantle there."

Sara came from the kitchen and Blount sensed that she would respond to the garrulousness in her parlor. He himself was startled by the change in the man since their meeting at the store; Nick's gaiety had a queer disorder to it.

"Do you like the painting?" she asked Nick.

"Cunts on a plane bore me, Sara."

Blount had to laugh, had to agree; the painting was not much more than a huge white field, in the center of which lay, soiled feet toward the viewer, a muscular and voluptuous woman approximately the color of bubble gum; *her* center, the center of the picture, was a distorted and pubic isoceles triangle.

Nick waggled his eyebrows at Sara until she relented enough to smile at his criticism of what Blount knew she considered to be beautiful. "You're impossible," she said.

Nick leaned over the table, spread one hand across the front page of the newspaper, and said to Blount: "Now you, I'll bet you love Edward Hopper."

It was Sara's turn to laugh. "Yes, yes, it's true," she said. "He likes all that profound silence. Wouldn't you both like something to eat?"

"Yes," Nick said, "vittles." And he sat down.

Later, as they ate the sweet toast, Nick fingered the newspaper spread out next to his coffee cup. "All the news that fits the Brahmin brain," he observed, something wistful in the set of his jaw; but it seemed a light comment, one that Blount could agree with easily enough, at least until Nick raised his coffee cup and Blount saw a hand tremor than was even worse than his own. Nick sipped, smiled with seeming pleasure at what had just heated his throat, put the cup down on the paper, and asked, "Don't you think it's time this paper called Nixon the cheap usurper he is?"

Blount was not particularly interested, but he said, "I don't think the editors will do that until he puts the east coast under martial law and executes all the members of the Harvard Club. Then it would be too late."

Nick laughed gloomily. "Not as unlikely as your little joke would suggest."

From the kitchen Sara called out, "Change the bloody subject. It's too nice a day for politics."

"Oh, right," Nick said, leaning toward Blount and winking. "You know something, I've written four screenplays in the last two years, and I'd like you to read them."

Blount was taken aback. "You write?" he asked stupidly. "I don't understand."

"No, that's not it." Nick looked genuinely morose — no longer impish or sly or ironic. "I'm trying to suck you into my confidence. I have a terrible problem and I need your help."

With this declaration he removed his cup from the newspaper and tapped a fat forefinger on the square of news photograph that Blount identified as the torn and smoking townhouse. He raised his eyes and saw that Nick's face was haggard, even afflicted.

At that moment Sara came from the kitchen; Nick immediately shook off his probable pain, returning to an expression that resembled appreciation of the tall woman who now stood near him. Blount took the opportunity to delay whatever unwanted confidence was about to burst upon him.

"Where's Oliver?" he asked Sara. "We're supposed to play ball."

"He's down at the Katzaris'," Sara said. "He made a point of telling me you had promised to play after lunch."

"Oh." Blount's options were dwindling. "Not if I'm working," he threw out, but Sara sat down at the table with them without answering; she began to read the second section of the paper, and Blount had just about decided that Nick's entire bit was an elaborate put-on, when the man began to talk again.

"See," he said, "there's this explosion, you can read about it right here; a house has been blown apart."

"I did," Blount said. Here we go, he thought.

Sara left off reading to stare at Nick as if he were offering some extraordinary commentary on the stinging habits of bees.

"The thing is," Nick continued, "Sylvia was in the house."

"Nick!" Sara cried. "You mean she's dead?"

The man winced. "No," he replied, "but her presence there, and her survival, have created a situation, the details of which aren't important, but she'll shortly be a fugitive from all the forces of law and order you can name. They *know*, or will know, she was there. So she's coming here."

He stopped, picked up his plate, and licked off what syrup remained with a tongue the color of raspberry sherbet.

Blount didn't know whether he recoiled because of the tongue or the information. "Why are you saying this?" he said, much more quickly than he had intended.

"Ain't it awful?" Nick observed with not a trace of his former pain. "Just listen. Think. The husband of a fugitive is in a peculiar position, even one like me who hasn't seen his wife for the two years she was in prison." He took out a cigarette and stuck it into his mouth.

Sara lighted it for him. "I thought Sylvia worked as a film cutter in New York," she said evenly.

"No," Nick said, "that was a lie."

"Cock and bull," Blount muttered, staring at the photograph and seeing for the first time the sourceless streams of water being directed into the hazed ruin. He knew the truth was being spoken, he knew the truth to be harmful, and he didn't want to hear another word.

"Look here, Nick, I don't want you to say anymore, you understand, I don't want anything to do with any of this, and your wife can be hung from the Washington Monument for all I care."

"Chris," Sara said.

"But Sylvia didn't *do* anything," Nick said.

Blount felt cagey. "What do you have, an elaborate radio hook-up with her?" Nick shrugged; it was maddening. "Don't give me that shit. You're leaving out too much. It doesn't make sense."

Nick shrugged again and raised his hands in a parody of supplication.

Rearing out of his chair so that it fell on the floor behind him, Blount shouted: "This is insane! Get out of my house!"

"Sit down, man," Nick said.

Jesus Fucking Christ, if he had another week-end like this he'd die. "Don't tell me what to do. Just say what you want of us in one clear English sentence or I'm going to break your legs." Blount became conscious of his own trembling just as he caught — out of the corner of his eye — Sara scowling darkly.

"No threats," Nick said. "That's a government game. All I want is for you to trust me, and to act like the individual you're supposed to be . . . fiction writer."

"Crap," Blount said.

"No," Nick said, "you're the one who wrote LOOSE ENDS, and if that new one over there is anything like it, you're not somebody who holds any brief for the state. It holds none for you. It's us against them, over and above any asshole concepts of social responsibility."

"Good speech," Blount said sarcastically, "but my vanity isn't so simple to light. All groups are dangerous. All groups are suspect."

"Shut up, Chris," Sara said, and then to Nick, "I trust you. Do you want some more coffee?"

Blount shifted from foot to foot, then leaned over to pick up the chair. He truly did not know what to do; not only had Sara split her love between Monica and him, but now she seemed to be offering them all up to some scheme of aiding and abetting that he could only begin to glimpse. What he saw clearly was his own children become wards of the state while he and Sara languished in their separate prison cells. He dropped the chair into place.

"I still want to know," he said to Nick's damnably candid face, "what it is you want us to *do*." Then he added, "I'm not a harborer of fugitives."

Nick grinned. Self-assurance? "I don't want you to do anything, Chris. Just know my problem, for now."

Aha, Blount thought, there it is. "When is she going to be here?" he asked.

Nick broke off his gaze and turned toward Sara, shaking his head rapidly. "I don't know that. Sylvia may be with another woman." He tapped the paper. "Or by herself. I don't know; it's a muddle."

"I'll say," Blount noted. "Okay," he said, "now that you've forced us to know the fix you're in, why don't you leave us be . . . and we'll try to develop some sympathy."

Sara was clearly irritated. "There's no reason we can't help out," she said. "It doesn't sound all that dangerous. Sylvia is this man's *wife*." The simple word was sufficient for her, Blount could see.

"Okay! Okay!" he shouted, waving his hands helplessly in the air.

Early Saturday afternoon Blount found himself dashing over the treacherous hills of his backyard after Oliver's wildly flung balls. The sharp sunlight of the morning had given way to an almost sultry haze of bluish cloud, and Sara had chosen not to continue hacking at her garden, but instead sat in a low-slung chair peering at Blount's weary galley proofs — somewhat listlessly, he thought. From time to time she tried to soothe Tom, who was miserable at not being able to play catch with his father and brother.

Blount, now dressed for exercise, sweating like a warthog and happier for it, had been relieved when his younger son awoke from his bee-stung nap alive; almost as relieved as he had been when Nick Winnoe departed as casually as he had come. In the yard, leaping and running and trying to direct his shots at Oliver's outstretched arms, Blount felt only fleeting spurts of the sheer mindless pleasure that usually came with ferocious exercise. In fact, he knew he was overdoing the entire show and he began to be conscious of himself as a kind of twitching marionette . . . a caricature of an athlete. Oliver kept missing the ball, but instead of running then at his father in order to protest that it was Blount's fault, the child would merely stop and gaze with a quizzical, near-amused expression on his delicate face.

Blount wished to stop his frenzy, if only because he thought the boy — or Sara — would soon begin to laugh at him, but to stop would mean facing the hard questions lurking like vicious spectators in the periphery of his sweaty vision. Questions about the Winnoes, about the Eatons, and even about his own trusting, faithless wife.

He noticed that Oliver had turned his back on the last throw, had simply walked away from the ball's careful trajectory. Blount stopped, hands on hips, breathing in jerks. His family seemed far-off. Stick-figures frozen in attitudes remote from him. A curse on them, on the infernal questions; a curse on himself for rolling with the punches, for agreeing to hire Monica, for ever leaving the safety and isolation of his house to go into a world that now appeared a jumble of senseless explosion and conspiracy.

He left nature. He left politics. He left history.

He left his family, left his wife's garden, left his idyllic backyard, and stalked trembling and sweating to his workroom, where he thought he might begin to purify himself with fiction — his third novel, A COMPLETE LIE.

No one spoke. No one looked. No one cared.

And Pablo Eaton had not brought his bicycle.

CHAPTER SIX

Oh, and what'll you do now, my blue-eyed son?

New York City
May 1, 1970

CROQUET, bird of night, left Sylvia intending a casual search for Stanley through the early electric difusion of Friday evening; he knew the fat and genial impressario Decatur Samson was in town, and Croquet thought time might be saved by putting Decatur on Stanley's trail. Questions about the morning bust and the true reason for Stanley's presence in the city wanted answers. An impossible task, perhaps — Stanley was no fool, whatever else he might be — and certainly one that was interrupted as soon as Croquet closed his apartment door on Sylvia and began to walk along the corridor toward the elevator.

"Pssst."

Acoustics conspired against him; it seemed that the sibilants had come from one of the cold white fluorescent assemblages above his bewigged head. He moved on.

"Psst," from behind him now, "Othello."

Halt. He wanted no confusion of roles in this place, and

so turned back not to Sylvia, but to Gjertrud, whose eye peered at him through the safety-chained crack of her apartment's door. "Open up, Gjertrud," he whispered, though Sylvia couldn't possibly hear. But Croquet could feel her on the phone to Nick, or to someone, just a wall or two away.

There stood Gjertrud dressed in a short silken robe the color of cantaloupe. "Goodness," Croquet said, not only affected by her unfettered, dependent breasts, but also by the large black and white photograph she held to the left of one jutting hip. A photograph so grainy that at first he mistook it for a grey abstraction of loops and whorls, but then recognized a navel, male, with a surrounding nap of tiny curling hairs. "What have you got there?"

"Nelson Algren's bellybutton," she said casually, lifting it up near Croquet's nose. "I'm doing a book of them. Will you come in?" She lowered her sample and indicated that he should pass by. Her breasts branched and flattened as she gestured, and when he came near, her mind radiated both a collection of innocent navels *and* something dark and pulsing. He grew wary. Polite he would be to this former lover, present friend; however, he needed no unnecessary complications to the present situation: Bip and Sylvia; Stanley's unpredictability; and the townhouse people about to offer up whatever would be their modest contribution to the ripples of the world.

Behind him she closed the door and redid and chain while he took a seat. He watched her come along the passageway toward him with a flashing of her efficient knees. She went to the divan opposite, sat, and folded her legs beneath her, the shimmering lapels of her robe pouching forward so that the distracting breasts became moot, and he was able to put his Sylvia-satiation in proper perspective.

"The bellybutton is the hickey of the soul," Gjertrud said with a straight face. Somberly.

"I hadn't thought of that."

Now, he knew, Sylvia was in the shower — an aural fact; he hoped she would find suitable clothes among the rag-tag of stuff left with him over the past year.

"Don't you think the timing is right for a book like this?"

Gjertrud asked. "Imagine a navel reference book . . . Algren, Capote, Miles Davis, Ginsberg, U Thant, Nick Winnoe . . . "

Croquet was shaken. She had never met Nick, not once. "Who?"

But she proceeded blithely. ". . . Bobby Zimmerman. And you. There's always room for versatile actors. What about right now? I've got floods, everything's all set up over there in the corner. Take off your shirt, drop your trousers, and I'll squeeze it off. But do I index you under Tommy Wicket or Mungo Croquet, or — what's the other one? — Edmund Silver?"

Now he understood; he had a full-breasted eavesdropper on his hands. Were the walls so thin? Could she possibly have heard Sylvia's entire soliloquy? All that about Nick, about the smuggling, the penitentiary, the somewhat melo-dramatic interpretation of his own mummer's politics? Was her mind full of images of black bombs flying willy-nilly? And he had — albeit flippantly — told her that very morning that he was going to blast the main offices of American Telephone and Telegraph . . . NOT SO, YOUNG LADY, NOT SO: I'M MERELY A DISINTERESTED OBSERVER OF CONTEMPORARY DELUSIONS . . .

But Gjertrud was not receiving. She only stared at him, waiting for an answer. Maddening. A cruelty came up like an unexpected clot of vomit, not quite choked back.

"Why don't you go all the way, and shoot cocks?" he asked. She blushed; he watched coolly as it spread down her neck. "Part art."

"What?" she said with a strangled look. Tears ready in their ducts. "Oh come on, don't make fun of me. It's damn lonely here, I only see you in the elevator. Why don't you come by anymore? I thought we used to do pretty well to-gether."

"I'm by now," Croquet said, more sharply than he knew she deserved. At this rate he'd be stuck with her just to pro-tect himself. A woman spurned . . .

She had bridled. "Sure you are. *After* screwing that babbling chick for two hours."

"It's none of your business."

Now the tears popped. "I don't want you to turn out to-to . . . be criminal."

"What did you use to listen, an upside-down water glass?" Croquet asked, then more angrily, "Or is there some sort of distant-sound amplifier in all that junk camera equipment?"

"Shit, Tommy." She drew the syllables out sadly. "Or whatever your name is, don't dump on me." Despite the tears her face was composed, boyish, earnest . . . even calculating, he thought. "Is there something I can *do?*" she asked. "I mean, I love you, and probably a lot more than what you've got in there."

Croquet considered the odds. Could he turn this accident to his advantage? Did he have any choice? If he rejected her now, might she take her bits and pieces of information to the authorities, as fitting vengeance? Possibly. He managed to smile, to put a joking twist on his words. "All right. You can join me in a very small conspiracy to interfere with a guy named Stanley Fielding's right to the pursuit of mischief."

She had leaned forward, clutching the robe against her throat; the breasts had come back to life. "This is a game, isn't it?" she asked hesitantly but with enough spirit to convince him that she was, for the moment, caught up in the idea of doing something, anything, with him.

"That depends on your point of view," he said. "But it's nothing serious. Get dressed. We'll take a stroll. See an old friend."

"What about the convict next door?"

"She has other things to do."

While Gjertrud was in the bathroom dressing — after touching lightly the skin of his cheek — Croquet went along to the entrance door, cracked it a quarter of an inch and waited for a glimpse of Sylvia's departure; no need to complicate matters with an accidental meeting of the two women. Perhaps she would even figure out what to do about Nick. Meanwhile, Croquet and Gjertrud would divine Stanley's whereabouts, or simply enjoy Decatur's speculations on the problem; Croquet's mind went no further into the evening, though vague twinges of warning had begun to percolate in its distant recesses. When his eye captured Sylvia in motion along the corridor, her rapid flat-footed shuffle, one of his own coats dwarfing her slight form, he felt the momentary anxiety shut itself down entirely. Sylvia bopped out of his sight, her head of ink black hair slightly tipped. Everything would be just fine.

Croquet shut the door, knowing that Gjertrud had come to stand right behind him. Without turning, he said, "There's something you ought to know about me."

Her breathing skipped a beat. "What is it?"

"I'm liable to spontaneously combust at any moment," he said lugubriously to the purple striations of her door. If his point was to warn and humor her at the same time, she responded only to the humor, as if he had offered her an opening she might trip happily through; she wrapped her arms around him and joined her hands above his heart. A ring of pressure. Her sharp chin punctuated the space between his shoulder blades.

"Where would Othello go?" she asked the hanging, bogus hair that he felt stirring with the air from her lips. "You smell like the desert."

Outside, they walked in the dusk, a time that laid a shroud of cleanliness and clarity over the quaint grime through which they passed. Croquet found beauty in smeary glass lit from behind, in neon signs reflected backwards in the sides of automobiles or in the tiny windows of parking meters, in the dark glasses of queerly bent passers-by, and in the guttered empty bottles of cheap sweet wine that had previously lit up a junkie's eye. He was pleased that Gjertrud had kept silent for a couple of blocks, and didn't mind when she finally spoke.

"Well, where're we going?" She placed a hand carefully in the crook of his elbow. "Can you find your friend with just your nose?"

He laughed. "No, I've got a date with the fellow. He's my manager, as a matter of fact." They covered another block. In the distance, Sixth Avenue showed up moving metal and headlights, and she paced beside him with her head bent forward; from her brain he received no more than vague curiosity of an ordinary blue color.

"Why do you want to find this Stanley?" she asked.

"He has access to some of the best Hollywood navels: from the fringe left all the way to Henry the K," he said.

She pressed his arm. "Come on, that was just a ploy to get you in the apartment."

"It wasn't Nelson Algren?"

"No," she said sadly, then brightening, "Frank Zappa's."

"Better," Croquet said. "The more dignity the better."

"I suppose." She pondered, and he sensed that the blue of her was darkening. "What do you really think of the President?"

"He dyes his hair and is driven alone over the freeways at fantastic speeds."

This broke the color. She laughed, for the first time. "I wish I knew you better," she said.

"Tommy Wicket, ma'am." He bowed in a sideways fashion. "A simple boy from Amarillo."

"Are we going here? The Riviera?" Gjertrud looked doubtfully at the cafe they had come to, that part of it which was a glassed cage on the sidewalk, packed with slouched and jawing customers. "I didn't know you went in for this sort of thing."

"I don't," Croquet said, "but when Decatur comes to New York he likes to gawk at as many highlife freaks as he can. What better place?"

"Is he here?"

"Yeah, see there." Croquet pointed through the glass. "That bald man with the red beard in the corner."

"Oh. Is he an anarchist, too?"

Croquet embraced her tightly with one arm, his mouth close to her ear. "Please don't talk like that. Decatur's just

91

a wealthy old boy from Dallas, and if you don't be nice to him I'll eat your bosoms." She gasped, not sure of this, probably afraid. Croquet threaded them through the mob of tables until they were able to confront the hunched form of Decatur Samson, who feigned ignorance of their presence until Croquet murmured, "How about some artichokes and conversation, Mr. Samson?"

At Croquet's question Decatur lost his slackness and seemed to fill with an enlivening gas. Amidst the curling disorder of his mouth-concealing beard, and beneath his slick dome, the skin of his face grew taut, even ruddier; he straightened up, smiling at Croquet, while his copper eyes whipped once over decidedly alien Gjertrud. "I'd adore," Decatur said a-doah, "an artichoke with drawn butter, but they aren't in season."

It was just a simple and friendly recognition code. "Not in these parts," Croquet said. "Gjertrud, this is Decatur. Get up and greet the lady, you clod."

Decatur ballooned out of his chair, almost knocking over the table with all five feet six inches and one hundred and eighty-five pounds of himself. He wore, as always, an immaculate light grey suit, a lavender shirt, and a string tie fastened with a heavy oval of silver and turquoise. "I'm pleased," he said, pumping Gjertrud's hand. "Would you all join me in a round of dranks?"

"Of course," said Croquet, securing two more chairs. "Trood here is a photographer," and he lightly squeezed the back of her neck as they sat down across from Decatur. "She does jobs around the country, record jackets and so forth." Decatur smiled broadly, waiting for the punchline, any hint as to how Croquet wanted him to relate to this stranger who nodded at him so solemnly. Croquet said, "She's an excellent listener, too." Gjertrud flushed, Croquet knew, but otherwise kept her composure. "Very discreet she is. I've seen her man her Nikon in a full room, as inconspicuous as a small wind."

"Ahh," Decatur exclaimed, apparently understanding that even though they were sitting with an accident, Gjertrud could be trusted, at least in this cafe conversation. "What'll you drink then, Miss Nikon? I'm having a tall cool glass of green wine. May wine, May day and all, you know."

"Some sweet vermouth," Gjertrud said, "with a twist."

Decatur beamed, waved his fist aloft. "There's that waitress. Hey there, Desdemona!"

Croquet did not turn but knew the waitress was behind him; felt her drooping Friday evening hauteur as she absorbed Decatur's order, to which Croquet added a request for a glass of vichy water.

"One vichy, one green, one ver-moot sweet," the waitress's voice reeded over the general hubbub.

"That's it, darlin'," Decatur crooned. He then massed forward until the leading edge of his beard nearly brushed Gjertrud's firm chin. "How do you like my friend Wicket? Idn't he something?"

"Do you mean," she replied calmly, "this pale gentleman?" She seemed to have decided that coyness would be safe enough.

Decatur barked with pleasure and leaned back in his chair with both soft hands spread out over his lavender belly, as though he were measuring its capacity. "I sure do. You should have seen him on stage last week. I tell you, his Othello had *power*. I mean, it was glorious!"

Gjertrud leaned forward on her elbows, cupped her hands around her mouth, and Croquet heard her pronounce distinctly "Faster than a flattened bullet . . . More powerful than a garden hose . . . Able to leap tall flowers with a single bound . . . It's M-U-N-G-O- C-R-O-Q-U-E-T!"

As Gjertrud began to spell out the name, Decatur performed an amazing double-take; consternation furrowed his dome, then melted as he was seized with a paroxysm of guffaws. Croquet, less demonstrable but believing the humor indicated she had completely abandoned nervousness and was indeed pursuing an aggressive policy, joined in, while hoping her jealousy of Sylvia was also well-buried.

Decatur, after catching his breath, said, "You've made my day. There ain't nothing sacred in this world, especially bleached-out actors with identity problems."

Croquet nodded at him and smiled.

"Okay, Decatur," Gjertrud declared, "now all you have to do is show me who *you* really are underneath." She darted out an arm and plucked his beard, but the cerise growth held fast, to her embarrassment, and she apologized.

While Decatur soothed Gjertrud for her gaffe, Croquet took a sip of the piquant water the waitress had brought. He was at once and again visited by vague twinges of warning; this time they took the form of fine plaster *bits* flung moiling over a surface of black Halloween paper. He saw himself, his actual blanched self, standing nearly-invisible in the dead center of a white maelstrom. But no meaning would come to him; the moving image remained only a scrim projection on his frontal lob as he watched Decatur sip his wine and practice his corpulent charm upon Gjertrud. If something wasn't quite right, somewhere, Croquet thought, then perhaps it was time to get down to business.

"You know," he interrupted, keeping his voice flat and factual. "Stanley's been in town since this morning." Decatur nodded, not surprised by any sort of transcontinental movement. Gjertrud stared into the red of her glass, polite but grasping every word, Croquet knew. "He's up to something; I don't know what. It may be perfectly harmless, but I'd like to find him."

Decatur assumed his thoughtful guise — a merry glower. "Thomas," he said, "what've you done with the lady con who phoned me up in Dallas a few days ago?"

"She's here, too . . . with Stanley's girlfriend," Croquet replied. "Sylvia's on her way to her husband."

"She's presently chained to *this* man's bed," Gjertrud volunteered, and Croquet winced at the small crack in her façade.

Decatur raised his eyebrows in reproof; he wanted no flashes of emotion either. "Curb your tongue there, would you," he said.

Her lips curled in aggravation. "You guys are being a little supercilious, don't you think. All this mumbo-jumbo.

Why don't you put an ad in the paper for Stanley? I think I'll go to the powder room, as they say."

"Wait, wait," Croquet said. "It's no big deal. I'd like to talk with him. That's all." As he said this he reached under the table and pressed his palm hard on her thigh. The contact, although meant to threaten and assure at the same time, precipitated — impossible as Croquet knew it to be — a far-off but palpable explosion: a *KRUMP* that penetrated even into the noisy cafe, for a short moment stopped all conversation, and caused Croquet to remove his hand from Gjertrud with such haste that it whacked the underside of the table and slopped from their glasses drops and splashes of vichy, vermouth, and green wine.

"Good lord," Gjertrud exclaimed, "what was that!"

"Back-fire," Decatur said.

"No," Croquet said. "Trouble."

And it was so: where before the transparent image had lightly overlaid his cafe vision, what he saw now was dark and hardened; his own form had been replaced by ghost-versions of Sylvia, Bip, others.

"Listen to me," he said firmly, quietly, grinding his teeth in the expectation that at any moment the grey rush of death would reach out and shut-off the image entirely, come shooting through the lath, plaster and stone that separated his mind from Sylvia's. "Decatur, you *know* what this is."

"I do hope you're wrong, buddy," murmured Decatur, showing the opal moons of his copper eyes.

"What are you talking about? what's wrong?" Gjertrud asked, more excited than afraid, it seemed.

"Shh," Croquet hissed. He had to get rid of her at once, and quickly decided to take the risk of sending her on a wild goose chase. "Would you get a cab over to Perry Street, would you do that for me?" he asked her.

"But what is it?"

He held her skeptical eyes and touched her thigh again. FOR A SHARE OF ME: DO IT! "Because I'm asking you to. Tell the cabbie to cruise by number eighteen, then go back over to your place. I'll meet you there."

She angrily took the five dollar bill he offered, started to rise. "I'll get an explanation?"

"Yes, you will," Croquet said. "Thank you."

"You're welcome, I guess." She left. Tall, elegant, and — Croquet knew — aware of being used.

Decatur gazed after her and made a subdued farting sound with his lips. "Was that wise?"

"No," Croquet allowed. "Would you get the waitress. Can you see Trood out there?"

"Yeah. There she goes."

Croquet bent across the table in order to be closer to Decatur's ear. "Facts and hunches, Mr. Samson. I saw Stanley this morning at Perry Street; he was high as a kite, and I had *not* asked him to come out from LA. Sylvia and Bip were busted — briefly — shortly after he arrived; he may or may not have had something to do with it, but now he's disappeared. The women are at Perry Street right now, or were, and there are some politicals down in the basement with their toys."

"Terrific."

"Stanley's the wild card," Croquet said. "He's so miswired he just may have done us up like this for a joke."

"Har-har," Decatur said, sucking air into his mouth. "Maybe I can find him through his New York connection, or a couple producers we both know. What if I do?"

Croquet hesitated; the unknowns were showing up like black holes in his mind. "Play it straight," he said. "Tell him there's been trouble, if he doesn't already know, and that he should go up to New England, to Vermont, and . . . meet Bip there. That's it."

"Is that safe? Wup, here she is. Check, please ma'am."

Croquet nodded, not at all sure that it was. "We'll see. If they're dead it won't matter."

Decatur closed his eyes. "May that not be so. I'll do my best to find him. Call you if I get on to anything."

"I may disincorporate within the hour," said Croquet.

"If that happens I'm going right back to Dallas. You wizard types give me the creeps."

Croquet smiled. The bill arrived.

"I'll pay this," Decatur offered as his bulk rose.

"Good luck," Croquet murmured.

"You too, buddy."

Back, back Croquet went under a darkening sky, through ultraviolet streets alive with shuffling promenade. He carried his curious lassitude like a sack of foam pellets, and was comfortable in the face of dangers he knew to be both actual and irrelevant: could he not escape from this claustrophobic world of dirt and blast with only a change of disguise and a ticket on a jet or a bus or a train? He could, and would if necessary. But if the politicals, who were victims of their *own* rhetoric, had accidentally imploded themselves on their collective stupidity, and Bip and Sylvia had survived, then Croquet's continuing obligation to the women would not permit him to leave them the terrifying sight of his own empty apartment. As he walked south, nearer both to his own place and the townhouse, the more certain he became that the two of them were on the move, had not been stopped.

The sirens came up, a mix of wolf whistles and long painful moans that faded to breathy sighs. A battered squad car went gunning down Sixth Avenue as he turned down 12th and began to jog for his building, not worried, but intent on heading off Gjertrud and providing succor for Bip and Sylvia should they make it to his apartment. Now he ran, long hair whipping about his eyes and cheeks.

Near the building he slowed, alert for signs of Gjertrud, but the block was quiet, dark, although a pair of headlights bore down on him from the north just as another *whoop-whoop* went up, then fell. He took cover just inside the entrance and waited for the headlights to prove themselves Gjertrud's cab. She failed to see him until after she had dismounted from the vehicle and walked through the doors. Not at all startled, she stopped, looked at him for several seconds, and then nodded. "You were right," she said. "I wish I'd had my camera." Her face was impassive, though he briefly sensed the scarlet wraiths that twisted and rose behind her clear eyes. "What now?"

"You go up," he said. "I'm going to stay here for a minute."

"Why?"

"Just go up," he said sharply. "I'll knock on your door."

She went into the bright foyer and walked toward the elevators. Sylvia was coming, no doubt about it, and if he could keep Gjertrud separated from the other two his logistics problems would be that much simpler. He turned to look at the street. Empty. But he heard the quick scuffle of Sylvia's walk and she rounded into the entrance, hugging the wall... ashen, tight, purposeful, until she saw him and abruptly seemed to lose her way, to deflate, to moan, "Mun—" before he could catch up her elbow, offer support, keep her from collapse. He embraced her and smelled ruin and fear.

"Are you alone?"

"Bip's coming." Sylvia was sobbing into his shirt front. "We had to separate, someone saw us."

A black man in a wide-awake hat passed by them without a glance.

"Don't talk," Croquet said. "Come on," and he began to lead her toward the elevator.

"Mungo, Bip's never been here!"

He stopped them, unsure. "You must have told her, dammit."

"Only the *block*," Sylvia wailed.

Croquet hustled them forward again.

But they were stopped cold by Bip's voice: "Hey white-folks, hold it!"

Croquet turned to see Bip out on the sidewalk, hands to hips, tented in something pink, glaring with a ferociousness undercut by the sprinkles of whiteness shot through her crown of hair. He motioned to her with the arm that was not around Sylvia, and Bip came to them radiating hatred that almost knocked him over with its brilliance. But they made a trio and hurried through the foyer, only to find Gjertrud still waiting innocently in front of the elevator. Trapped. So be it, he thought, chopping the UP button.

"I already did that, Tommy," Gjertrud said, possessiveness like a mild frost in her voice.

Bip and Sylvia ignored her. The doors opened, they all stepped in, Croquet pushed 3, and as the doors approached one another he was relieved to have them all boxed for a moment. UP. Bip continued to glower; next to her, almost leaning on her, Sylvia carefully watched the floor, and he suffered briefly the illusion that he could see her skull be-beneath the film of skin on her drawn face. Gjertrud stood in the corner opposite him, seemingly in full control. Faced with the three, his heart — temporarily a safe, reeded cave — could accommodate them, one and all.

"Who's she?" Bip broke the silence, thrusting her chin crudely at Gjertrud. "Calling you *Tommy*."

Gjertrud's glance trembled; her chin pebbled like a child's. Croquet felt sure that she would manage to keep a dignified silence, but no: "What about you, honey? I can guess Sylvia. Are you the bodyguard?" Gjertrud hesitated, glum and feisty, then suddenly a cruel brightness came over her. "No, you're Bip, the one they *set up* to hold little Sylvia's hand in prison. Am I right?"

Devil take it! Bip catapulted Croquet a look that would have withered a buzzard.

"What does she say!" Bip shouted.

Sylvia placed a restraining hand on Bip's threatening forearm, and the elevator reached the third floor; the cracking door temporarily relieved the thoroughly wrongheaded tension.

As they moved into the corridor, Croquet touched Sylvia's leather-jacketed back, and said, "Easy does it, folks."

Gjertrud walked ahead, searched her bag for a key. Bip stalked behind her, the pink cape flouncing idiotically at the backs of her bare thighs. Sylvia clenched Croquet's arm, forcing him to bend his ear close to her mouth. "Three corpses, lover," she whispered with a laziness that must come from shock.

He hushed her, indicating by pressure that she should go along with Bip to his own apartment door, but he stopped behind Gjertrud, who was fumbling with her key. "I want you to come to my place."

"No," Gjertrud said, "let me wait. You take care of that big woman first. I don't want her to kill me."

Fair enough; it was a reprieve of sorts. "All right," he said to her. "You shouldn't have said what you did. I'll quiet them down and come after you later." Gjertrud did not apologize.

He shepherded Sylvia and Bip into his apartment. At the sitting end of the narrow room he switched on a single lamp and closed the curtains. Sylvia immediately lay down on the couch, but Bip stood like a tree in the middle of the rug, clearly intent upon bile and accusation.

How to disarm her? "Would you like some other clothes? Aren't you hungry?" he asked.

She showed her teeth. "You're really one incredible dude, you know it." She shook her finger at him, rocking to and fro on her bare feet. "We come out here in good faith and there you are at the airport got up like Marco Polo, watching yourself on the teevee." Sylvia stirred; Croquet frowned. "Next thing, we're thrown in jail for nothing, then we're almost offed by kids who can't tell a stick of dynamite from a cherry bomb, and now some fancy-ass *New Yorker* insults me, sez you had me sent-up on purpose. So please, Mister Croquet, let's don't waste our time talkin' about fucking *duds*."

"Oh, Bip," Sylvia said mournfully, raising one dusty leg into the air and letting it fall back on the couch with a soft plop. "Let it be." She looked at Croquet. "Were you at the airport?"

"He sure was, sister. Narcissus himself. I swear, I think he arranges everything just for his own jollies. But this time he's bought a load of bloody murder." Bip's eyes had not left his; her mind was practically bursting with images of Stanley. If he were to tell her that the man she loved had probably gone bonkers, would she stay on, or would she bolt screaming into the streets?

"Bip," he said as gently as he could, "I had nothing to do with your arrest two years ago; it was Stanley's *error* and you know it; he burned you and you supposedly forgave him."

She grimaced but kept quiet.

"The rest was just a simple arrangement: we made sure you were sent to Terminal Island. That's all. It's the truth."

Bip seemed to lose the physical support her outrage had provided; she collapsed backward into a chair and wiped a hand across her lips, mumbling syllables he couldn't hear. Her eyes were fixed on Sylvia now and her face had gone to plagued affection.

Sylvia sat up, nervously pulling at her rucked skirt. She looked dazedly at the fish, at the bed beyond, then seemed to gather herself by shaking her head quickly from side to side. She looked directly at him; he was receiving nothing but white noise. No contact. Her face was clear and she was as still as light.

"You fucked up, Mungo, you really fucked up," she said quietly. "First the smuggling, then whatever you've done to Stanley, and now . . . this."

"Do tell," Bip said.

Croquet raised his hands in protest. "Who saw you?" he asked; he'd get command of this yet.

"One nutty lady," Sylvia said sullenly. "She thought I was the daughter."

"And who was in the basement?"

"The daughter. And a guy. It must've been . . . shit—"

"What?"

Bip finished: "The third one made it downstairs and was coming out on the street when the whole shebang fell on him."

"The idiots," Croquet said.

Sylvia whispered dully, "How can you be so monstrous?" Her blank, exhausted face didn't change until she saw him shrug.

"I'm not responsible," he said.

Every muscle in her face twisted and contorted. "Suppose,

just suppose it had been three children?" The words were hot and stuck to one another.

"It wasn't," he said quickly.

"My God." Sylvia looked at him for a long moment, more composed now. "You're a cold cold *nothing*. I want to get out of here."

"Right," Bip said. "Let's find Stanley and jump on the plane; at least his fiascos don't end up with snuffed people."

"We can't," Sylvia cried; her ability to calculate the future was apparently not impaired. "No. The lady's description will lead the cops right to our bust this morning, then they'll follow it back to California, and pretty soon they'll know."

"They'll hassle Stanley."

"And Nick," Croquet said, watching Sylvia flinch.

"But not *you*," Bip said bitterly.

"We have some time," Croquet said. "It's Elaine Freeman who's the fugitive."

"And an unidentified fat Nee-gro companion," Bip added, jerking her head defiantly.

"Until they put together all the little pieces of flesh," Sylvia muttered, then louder, "I hate all this figuring, these plans. It's so dumb, Mungo. So goddamn unnecessary." She fell back against the couch. "I'm sorry I balled you, you know that." Her voice rose wildly in his ears. "I shouldn't have done that!"

CHAPTER SEVEN

She's an artist, she don't look back.

New York/New England
May 1-2, 1970

SHE — her hair now a bright peroxide blonde — came into the late Friday evening jostle of the Port Authority Bus Terminal. You would recognize the swift, flat-footed gait of the young woman as she made her way among the military uniforms, baffled travelers, and finger-popping gents. Her gaunt body was enveloped in corduroy trousers, much too large, a pale blue T-shirt, and a green poplin jacket with the sleeves rolled back twice to give her hands freedom. From one shoulder hung a scarred musette bag, and on her feet were soft-soled deerskin boots that laced up her shins and bloused the trousers like odd knickers — Croquet's last offering to her.

Alone, weary, but operating on the reserve energies of vexation, shock, and the trembling need for prudence, Sylvia had by necessity foresaken Bip to the opaque plans and devices of either Croquet or Stanley (should he show up), and Sylvia was now determined to travel the remaining distance to her husband, no matter how foolish and hazardous this last leg of her journey from Terminal Island Penitentiary might be. With Croquet's money she bought from the clerk a one-way ticket to Brattleboro. The bus, a wretched local to Springfield, Massachusetts, would leave in ten minutes, would take more than five hours, and so — it seemed — what with changing busses in Springfield, she would not see Nick until after the sun had risen on Saturday morning.

On the departure platform, corraled by iron piping, she stood eating a candy bar amid the roar of the elephantine busses and the reek of worn oil and noxious exhaust. In the dimness of the yellow plastic light-bars she felt safe, innocuous, even patient, as she rested an elbow on the greasy pipe and waited for the driver to admit her line into his vehicle. In front of her a black man in a batik dashiki cleared his throat and spat over the railing at the front tire of the bus. Accurately: a blessing on this journey. Because his back was turned to her she could see that beneath the short tail of his shirt he was clenching and unclenching his buttocks in spasms that made the cloth of his pants ripple and fret. She stared, tonguing the film of sweet chocolate from her teeth, until her head was full of nothing but the twitching rhythm of the man's nervous, bewitched ass.

No need to think for now; no need to regret abandoning Bip, though it had been absolutely necessary; no need to pay heed to the clot of pain and guilt that she knew she could activate at a moment's notice, like a quick flick of her tongue at a rotten tooth. No need to bring into focus the mauled, bloody torso that hung in a cold recess of her brain. No. As long as she could be absorbed by what was happening in front of her nose she would be all right. She could stand it. But her reverie was broken by the long hissing sigh of the opening door. The dark man moved forward and she with him. -

Croquet's dull rote spun through her mind as she handed the driver her ticket to be punched: don't fraternize with strangers; don't allow yourself to register in anyone's recollection; don't make telephone calls, or write letters, or send telegrams; don't become party to, witness of, or participant in an accident. How in God's name would she avoid that? The driver holed her ticket, tore part of it for himself, and then she climbed aboard and took a seat near the cockpit. The dashiki man had disappeared.

Her gut began to ache and she felt the trembling of her shoulders and even her torso underneath the jacket and T-shirt. Here she was a convicted felon who'd done hard time, and now this cramping definition would expand to *fugitive;* fugitive not only from the law but perhaps from Croquet, who had said, when he handed her the freshly-typed ID, "Go to Nick if you have to, Syl, but if you stay more than forty-eight hours you're dead. The FBI will be on him as soon as they make the connections. Nick has friends in that town; you can trust them, though they won't be safe for long either. Don't count on anything or anybody. If I have to I'll come up there with Bip and snatch you all into Canada."

And she, who thanks to him had become Margaret Woolf of Sunapee, New Hampshire, had replied in harsh prison tones, "I'll take care of myself, Mungo . . . whatever your creepy name is." Her feelings about him as she left the apartment, leaving Bip, had been and were now an anxious mix of contradictions. Condemnation, rage, and a watery, stupid love for the man who struck her as a murderer no matter how hard she listened to his talk of accident and ineptness, and no matter how sharply and, yes, sweetly, her body remembered the tenor of their afternoon in bed.

So, was Nicholas C. Winnoe, her husband by law for almost three years now, her last refuge — and a hopeless one at that? No, not so simple. She was after no refuge, wanted only to discover if she still had a husband *in fact,* wanted to know if the vague poltergeist he had become would or could incorporate and carry her into a life somewhere beyond the reach of Croquet's lurid influence. What an idiot I am, she thought; Nick is no more than an unkind and blustering cynic — in cahoots with Croquet for reasons no more complicated than dumb adoration. Her stomach convulsed and she suddenly felt it gourd hard, its contents rising to her gorge. The chocolate came bitterly into the back of her throat.

Conspiracy, horrible accident and mutilation, betrayal:

a slimy mess. Hadn't Sylvia betrayed Bip by leaving her to Croquet? Wouldn't he manipulate her in ways that Sylvia couldn't begin to fathom? Somehow make her a fall-guy for Stanley? She shivered and swallowed the dreg of vomit. If Bip got hurt Sylvia knew she would be to blame.

The bus driver hopped the stairs and stood next to her, glaring the length of the aisle, counting the dozen or so passengers. He scribbled on his clipboard, mounted his seat, ground the machine into reverse and handled it through the dark byways of the terminal with bold circular gestures that at least gave Sylvia the reassurance of plain motion.

At sunrise she stepped to the tarmac of a gas station on the outskirts of Brattleboro. She had discovered, waiting for the bus north in Springfield, that the vague cramps out of New York and through Connecticut were due as much to the onset of her period as to emotional and physical strain. She had found a restroom tampon machine, but now, standing alone and in pain beside a deserted Route 5, the bus gone on, she realized a predicament not foreseen during the long trance of her journey: there was no bus station. No haven. The gas station gloomed at her, shut up tight; so, too, the restaurant across the way. No roof, no direction, and no new stopper for her guts.

In the feeble early light she could see, off down the road to what was probably New Hampshire, a black railroad bridge that spanned the highway. On its face, in gracefully-looped white lettering, were the words:

ANNIE SUROWIEC I LOVE YOU

She was surprised to find that this rural graffiti gave her a small jolt of pleasure; even then she began to fret about the possibility of the police. She needed no smirking constable to roust her off of this dead road. As she ran the image in her mind — 'I'm on my way to Annie's, officer. Only to Annie Surowiec's for some succor in the wilderness.' — Sylvia felt as if a heavy brass weight were dependent in her lower belly, a weight that made her stoop as she began to walk north along the highway. But immediately she knew it would be wiser to remain where she was, with at least the possibility of an alibi that she was just waiting for the next bus to Montreal.

Shit, her teeth were chattering.

A car appeared off to the south. She turned back for the gas station, walked slowly toward the pumps and leaned with what she hoped would seem casual purpose against one of them. The car came on fast — no cop, she decided — with a rough whine that made it sound more like a piece of heavy equipment than an automobile. Some sort of van, dark and spattered with mud, it slowed for the intersection and turned right. She could see the shadowy outlines of two figures in the cab. Hair. Men or women. The driver turned a face to her briefly, indistinct, but kept the vehicle moving at speed on down the hill and underneath Annie's bridge. A blue van, now gone out of her sight.

What had she hoped for? A kind of Hollywood luck that would have the two of them recognize her as someone in need of kindly aid? As someone who required a ride of only eleven or twelve miles (she believed, because Croquet had told her so) to the place where she might finally lie down and give way to tears. Barf on such luck, she thought. She wished for a simple suitcase and a respectable dress — a proper front for the constable and the Brattleboro holding tank. Screw it.

Another car. This time it came slowly up from the bridge to the intersection. The van. It turned onto the tarmac and pulled up beside her.

The driver, a blonde man with a light wispy beard, regarded her impassively. "Hello, sister," he said. Sylvia could not see his passenger. "Are you waiting for Merlin?"

"Who?" she asked.

His smile came and went. "Just my little joke. You know, no busses come by here until eight o'clock."

Sylvia made her decision. "I'm not waiting for the bus," she said evenly. "I need a ride . . . to Windsor."

"Where've you come from?"

"New Hampshire."

"I was there once to get my dog."

"Can you help me?"

The man's pale blue eyes smiled at her. He turned his head and exchanged words with the other person. Over the clatter of the engine she heard the higher tones of the other's response, but no individual words. The driver's face swung back to her. "Go round back, Margaret," he said.

Sylvia hesitated, then wavered. All right, Croquet's juggling fingers had reached even this far north, as he had promised, she supposed, but she felt suddenly so listless, so without a will of her own that she could not move.

"Come on, sister."

She thought of fainting; she saw the bloodied lathing of the townhouse; she saw a bowl of hot vegetable soup; she saw Nick falling through space into treetops . . . then knew it was herself falling . . . and when the driver lifted her from the oily tar as if she were a numb child, she made no protest. He passed her through doors and deposited her on something soft and fluffy. He wrapped her in a lightness that smelled like ashes. "She's so skinny, Pablo," a woman's voice said, an altitude away.

There was a smell of hay and old manure. She opened her eyes, and above her slots of sunlight glinted between the ill-fitting boards of an old barn, and she knew herself to be hot and sweaty, covered with a blanket and lying on a pile of loose hay.

A rooster crowed from somewhere below. There was a

clattering sound, then a woman's voice — different from the one in the van — moving away, calling "Chick, chick, chick."

Sylvia threw off her covering and, rising from the hay, felt that the crotch of her trousers was sticky with blood. She removed her light jacket and tied it about her waist, then walked the length of the loft and peered around the edge of the half-open door. Ten feet below, in a dusty space between the barn and a drooping white clapboard house, a short woman in a robe was feeding a few red chickens with fistfulls of stuff that she fetched from a bucket slung over one arm.

From this height Sylvia could see no other houses; only green rocky meadows scattered willy-nilly among long, darker swatches of woods that in the far distance became the gentle pulse of old hills. Well, she thought, I am somewhere, and I'm safe.

The woman moved slowly toward the house flinging the feed as if she wanted to be done with it as quickly as possible. Her hair, clipped short, the color of old hay, was mussed, and her downcast face in profile seemed petulant, or wounded. When she reached the stoop she turned and looked up at Sylvia, as though she had known all the while she was being spied upon.

"Are you okay?" she asked. The neutral question, spoken quietly, carried easily across the chicken yard and up to the loft.

Sylvia gave the hay door a push so that it swung out and clapped against the barn's siding. "I guess," she said. "May I come down from here? I've got the curse and I'm pretty messy."

The woman put one hand to her brow and screwed up her face in what appeared to be confusion. With the other hand she put down the bucket and clenched the robe over her chest. "Do whatever you want," she said finally.

"Where am I then?"

"Bristol West . . . near Windsor."

"It's nice here," Sylvia offered, suddenly so cramped she had to grab the door frame.

"We like it," the woman said, removing her hand from

her forehead and smiling nervously. "Come on in the house and I'll get you some tampons." She picked up the bucket. "Pablo said to feed you." Then she went inside.

Sylvia returned to the hay mound, found her boots, the musette bag — all worldly goods accounted for — and as she was lacing the boots caught a whiff of herself, a strong but not unpleasant mix of sweat, blood and hay dust. Carrying the bag and the quilt, she went down a rickety staircase into the must and gloom of the barn's main floor, and outside, where the full clarity of the air gave her a measure of the calm she was looking for.

Inside, after Lucia Eaton had introduced herself and agreed to call Sylvia Margaret, and after this strangely kind but uneasy woman had pointed out the bathroom and Sylvia had found what she needed, the two women moved shyly about the kitchen. Lucia prepared coffee and muffins. In her ignorance Sylvia didn't know what Lucia might have been told, and she was reluctant to mention Nick, or what plans might have been made for her. But she could feel his presence among the debris and bottles of the kitchen. Lucia set the breakfast in a cleared space on the table and indicated that Sylvia should sit, but her restlessness and the congestion of her insides wouldn't allow it, so she took one of the muffins and walked back and forth in the room. She found herself drawn obsessively to the window above the sink and to all the free space that she could see; the lovely, rolling landscape.

"Do you own all that?" she asked Lucia.

Lucia came to stand beside her at the sink, as if relieved to be asked so simple a question. "Goodness, no," she said. "We just have a couple of acres down on the other side of the house, to the pond and the graveyard," and more confiding, "That's where my daughter Issy is, down at the pond."

"Oh." They gazed out of the window for a while. Sylvia felt that both of them were soothed by it. "You have one child?" she asked.

Lucia looked wistfully sad, until her face fractured into a smile. "Yes, she's nine. Pablo's had a vasectomy."

Sylvia turned and leaned her hip against the counter, folding her arms casually. "Really? How do you feel about that?" She was beginning to enjoy the simple mundaneness of this kitchen chat.

Lucia pondered. "Well, I can tell you it makes adultery something to think twice about." She made this pronouncement in such a deadpan way that Sylvia didn't know whether it was a joke or some mournful complaint, but when another smile rose onto Lucia's face and she actually chuckled low in her throat, Sylvia returned the smile. Lucia said, "Men are goats, you know." Still, the toughness seemed feigned, put on momentarily for what Lucia believed Sylvia *was*. No matter.

Feeling looser, Sylvia went for her coffee cup and took a hot sip. "Do you know Nick very well?" she asked. His name came so easily to her tongue that she was surprised.

"Oh, yes," Lucia said. "He's Pablo's best friend. I love to hear him talk." She paused. "You haven't seen him for a long time."

Sylvia's belly tensed for a moment. "No, not since I went to prison," she said, more harshly than she had intended.

Lucia looked alarmed and tried to cover it by going to the stove for more coffee. When she came toward Sylvia with the pot her eyes had begun to tear. "Please," she began to say, but then stopped as she poured more coffee. "I-I just don't want to know too much about this business. I'm sorry . . ."

"It's all right," Sylvia said. "I know I'm disturbing you and you're good to take me in. Where's your husband?"

Lucia seemed relieved to return to the safety of domestic questions. "He took Jep into town, I think; that damn dog broke his tooth on a rock, has a toothache, we finally figured out."

Sylvia laughed. "And the woman with him when he picked me up this morning?"

"That was Monica," Lucia said. "She's around here some-where. Maybe with Issy. She's a very smart girl."

"Who?" Sylvia asked.

"Monica," Lucia said complacently, as if she had already proved Monica's smartness. "She lives here with us. Babysits Issy and the Blount kids."

Sylvia finished her coffee and stretched. "Why don't we go outside. I like the air here," she said.

Lucia's eyes narrowed. "You think that's all right?"

Sylvia shrugged, feeling reckless, uncaring. "Yeah, why not?"

After Lucia left the kitchen, Sylvia washed her dishes, thinking of nothing more than the task before her; she felt that if she could keep moving, preferably in the sunlight, things would take care of themselves. Nick would appear when he appeared. Don't push it.

The screendoor banged in the midroom and a dark-haired child ran through the kitchen, tossing back a cool "Hi" as she made for the hallway down which Lucia had disappeared a few moments before. The door sounded again and into the room stepped a long-necked girl wearing a halter and shorts.

"Hello, Margaret," she said with complete self-possession. "You're looking better. I'm Monica Baldi." There was no ex-pression whatsoever on her soft face.

"Thanks for picking me up," Sylvia said, vaguely intimi-dated.

"It's nothing. You've eaten?" Sylvia nodded. "You can't stay here. Pablo wants you to get your gear and take the bicycle in the barn down the mountain to Chris Blount's house. Nick can catch up with you there. He may be there now. The thing is to move right away from here."

Sylvia's shaky calm evaporated, leaving a fine dust of anxiety that she tried to conceal from the forceful girl. She remembered the man who had shouted at them from the street outside the townhouse, and now the feelings of being prodded and planned-for returned like small, unpleasant charges going off in her heart. "I'm on the underground railroad," she said weakly.

112

Monica allowed herself a half-smile. "I guess," she said in a whisper as Lucia Eaton came into the kitchen buttoning up her jeans.

Sylvia had never ridden such a bicycle as this one Monica had said belonged to Chris Blount. She coasted what must have been more than a mile before she understood the relationship between the small levers on the frame and the toothed front and rear sprockets. Still, the effort to span the minor up-grades produced such slips and clunks that she was sweating and irritated by the fourth mile. She knew, though, that it wasn't so much the difficulties with the silly machine as it was the anticipation of Nick and the Blounts.

When Monica had finished giving her directions and Lucia had gone off with the child, Monica said, "Don't mind Chris Blount; he'll come around and maybe give us a hand . . . But right now he's like a treed porcupine whose quills won't shoot. Never could, in fact. But Sara, look well on her; she's the queen of Sheba." Sylvia had not understood, hadn't paid much attention in her eagerness to get the unfamiliar bicycle rolling, but now — stopped at the roadside to rest — she wondered what further complications she was about to encounter. The sun, now fading behind a bluish haze, cooled her sweat, and as she began to roll again, pedaling confidently over the pocked road, she felt that since she'd gotten the hang of the bicycle, the rest would speed by her as easily as the trees whipped along the edges of her vision. She would simply watch these people as if they were characters in some slow, rural film . . . until Nick showed himself, revealed what was in store for her, for them.

Down, down she went. The thick maples were broken more and more by farms, houses, a sawmill, someone's fur-niture making enterprise. When the speed became too much for her she squeezed the brakes in quick spurts as Monica had instructed, slowing in time to make the right hand turn into the Blount's Silver Birch Road.

Lightly, almost dreamily, she walked the bicycle up the driveway. When she reached the garage she put down the kickstand and allowed the thing to lean; she untied her bag from behind the saddle and looked about her. From somewhere she heard a child's voice, yelling, "TOM!"

She walked slowly to the porch door and stared through the screen until she could make out figures moving over the lawn on the backside of the house. She went through the door, crossed the porch, and after dropping her bag let herself outside, into a light that was a delicate mixture of soft yellow and green, all overlaid with the grey dome of sky. Two children, one tall and gawky, the other short and thick, were playing ball, and a ways beyond them a woman worked in a garden. Sylvia stopped. She felt as invisible as an invading gas; she did not want to interrupt the peace of what was before her, not at all. How simple to step backwards and vanish, but the woman — Sara Blount — was beckoning to her, and Sylvia discovered herself moving toward her as if she had lost all will. When they embraced, Sylvia knew the world had stopped.

On the grass close to Sara, both of them cross-legged, the boy Tom gurgling between them, Sylvia watched the other woman's wide mouth as she spoke with graceful and easy assurance. Sara's attention had a simplicity that was both flattering and pleasing, and now Sylvia's entire body felt infused with a languor that no drug had ever produced. It was a matter of listening to someone Sylvia realized she had known always as a dignified old friend.

"When I was a girl in Bridgeport," Sara was saying, "I fell into the good company of an Irish Catholic priest named Tom Conover." She reached out a slender, bony hand and touched her child on the end of his small nose. "Maybe he was thirty, I was seventeen. He was ruddy and brown-haired and as hefty

114

as Nick. He had a way of speaking that made me shiver just to hear his voice in the confessional or when he said mass or when he took me sailing on the Sound, after my mother and father decided he was 'better for me' than the rich kids I'd been hanging around with."

Sara interrupted herself to tell the other boy, Oliver, not to throw his ball against the back of the house, too near the windows that gleamed blackly out at them.

"Father Conover, Father Conover," she resumed. "His name seemed to plant itself in my heart from the beginning — beating through my body as I sat in school with the dry Sisters, or sewed him a heavy wool shirt as blue as his eyes, that he could wear in private for reading; he wore it the day we went sailing, I think to show me he wasn't afraid to appear in mufti, though he kept his collar on underneath, and the black coat in a plastic bag right between us in the cockpit."

Sylvia laughed easily, sure that she knew how the story would end.

"He told me about Ireland until I felt I'd been born there myself — a colleen after his own heart, you might say. And also what to read; and what was worth believing and what was not in Mother Church; and how to see the world as a struggle for love against the kind of easy, tough cynicism I'd already begun to see in my arrogant little friends. He was wonderful.

"And after he made love to me in the boathouse when we got back from the sail — it was raining and we were wet and it was already dark by the time we got the boat stored away — he just went away from the city, as if he'd never been there at all, and in my shock or grief or whatever it was, I came to believe that he had been sent to show me the right way, to make me know that I didn't have to stay in my narrow world one bit longer than necessary. So, the next year I went to Boston to college and never looked back."

Sara Blount lowered her eyes and brushed her palms across one of her bare knees as though, Sylvia thought, she were touching chamois.

"I've known men like that," Sylvia said, a little more wistful than she'd intended. "It's amazing, or it can be."

115

Sara tossed her dark hair in a way that was almost dismissive. "And women," she suggested. "My friend Monica has the same quality that Father had — clear perception through love is what it is — even though she's young and part of a world that most likely causes him, if he's still ticking, to pray fanatically." She laughed, then said without warning, "Politics are boring, and I don't much care about yours, but I do want to know that you aren't going to hurt my children or me or my husband. You and your friends."

Sylvia involuntarily reached out to the other woman, her response spilling from her mouth as quickly as she could make it. "No!" and her voice cracked as she went on, "I'm not. I won't stay here any longer than I have to. Please, Sara, don't worry."

But the other woman was looking into the middle distance as if she hadn't heard, as if she didn't *need* to hear.

Oliver came across the lawn, kicking at the ground with his tennis shoes. He stood in front of them and dropped his soccer ball on Tom's head. It bounced into Sylvia's lap.

"Oliver," Sara said, coming out of her reverie to see the unfazed Tom.

"Mom."

"What is it?"

"Can I get Dad?"

"No. What for?"

The boy pouted for a few seconds. "I thought we could play some more."

"He's working, honey. Let's leave him alone. Why don't you go down to the Katzaris' and see what Van is doing?"

"No."

"Well, then go fix yourself something to eat."

After Oliver left, and until Tom turned cranky, they spoke into the aura of suspended enchantment that Sylvia believed Sara had willed around them. Sylvia told her something of her own past — of college, of Nick and the bridge and her own transformations, and of the psychic jolts of the prison. But she did not mention Croquet, or Bip for that matter; it was not out of fear so much as a desire to avoid that which she knew Sara would not permit, details that might someday curl back and wallop her new friend. Sara seemed made only for beauty.

Their colloquy ended abruptly with the slam of the porch door, and Sylvia looked up to recognize Nick Winnoe as he emerged from the porch and moved across the lawn, like a dark, gay proboscis monkey, you would have thought. No Father Conover arriving here, Sylvia knew.

She inhaled a great draught of the good air, summoning the energy necessary for dealing with this stranger, this slob, this swarthy invader heading right for her. His eyes shone out of a face held in the heavy repose she remembered meant that he was excited, ready to spring into any situation that promised mix-up, wit, or sexual possibility.

"Syl," he growled from ten feet away, and that was when she leapt up and flung herself at him. She never knew she would, but when they hit and embraced, the old impression of his girth, the smell of Camels now mixed with an oily grime, returned in a whoosh that was like losing breath. She was crying. She kissed his neck and felt him tighten his arms briefly about her back, then loosen them so that he could step away, frowning but beaming, and say, "You skinny twat, how the hell are you?"

It was him all right.

Sara was a definite presence behind her. "I'm good, Nick," she said. "It's good to be here." She turned toward Sara, who smiled, Tom hugged to her breast.

"I'll leave you guys alone," she said, climbing up from the ground.

Something in her tone caused gooseflesh to rise on Sylvia's bare arms — a slight edge that seemed to say, 'Watch out.' As Sara walked away from them Sylvia removed her hands from Nick's and swiped her hot eyes.

"Thank you, Mrs. Blount," Nick called out after Sara, "we're grateful." Then he moved closer to Sylvia and touched her chin with his hand, whispering, "Your hair looks terrible, but on the whole I'm impressed." He took her hand and they began to walk away from the house and towards the meadows that began a rocky rise at the edge of the yard. Sylvia wasn't fooled by his bluff; the man who held her hand and had willingly matched his pace to her own was pleased to see her, and if he was a bit nervous and wary around the eyes, what more could she expect; he had a lot to answer for. And so did she.

She raised her head at him, trying to offer him a look that showed both her pain and her new pleasure. His goddamn eyes twinkled.

"I've had a hard trip," she said.

"I know you have." He shook his head and snorted. "Messes, Syl, messes. You should've told me when you got out."

The anger surged, then fell back before she could figure out how to voice it. "I tried to," she said quietly. "You should have written me, you know." It was no accusation, just a pretty little fact which he seemed not to have heard as he walked slowly beside her.

"It's time to regroup, choose a new leader. Othello hath murdered sheep."

"Nick!" Her fingernails scraped at his palm as the vivid image of Elaine Freeman's body was riven clear through her brain.

"I'm kidding, kidding," he said hurriedly. "Jollity is supposed to solve everything." He had stopped and was tightly gripping her hand to prevent injury to his own. She could read nothing in his nebulous brown eyes.

"It's uncaring and morbid," she said. "You always pulled that crap. We aren't in a joke anymore, Nick."

He let go her hand and slung his arm over her shoulders. They began to walk again, and because she sensed he had shut-up because he agreed with her, she put an arm around his girth, was content to rest her fingers on the mild fat of his waist as they rose up and away from the Blount household behind them. She thought/hoped that all the rest would wait until they had gotten used to the shifts and bumps of each other, but he just couldn't leave words alone.

"Croquet says you really laid into him," he said.

"I was hysterical." She half-believed it. "I know it was

an accident . . . but even Bip saw how queer his relationship to those people in the townhouse was. As if his fun was to be only what they needed him to be. It stinks."

Nick was not looking at her; he stared toward the top of the hill as though someone might be waiting there for them.

After a long silence, he again snorted, and said, "No queerer than with anyone else. Did he get in your pants, Syl?"

His tone was flip, but she froze. Halted their forward motion. Was it all going to come down to the simple but horrible matter of jealousy? Christ, she'd whack him with the truth, and if they couldn't get beyond it, then to hell with him; she would go back down to the clear reality of Sara Blount.

"Yes," she said softly. He raised one eyebrow in the gesture of mockery that was always meant to cover surprise. "Yes. I wasn't any less in that creature's power than you are, or Stanley, or poor Bip. Do you think I know what to do when he stands there *looking* at me?" They had turned to face the house. "I don't know what he is, a gamester, a chameleon, a wicked little kid, but I do know I wanted him after two years of being without, and—" the bitterness welled up of its own accord and splashed towards him— "two years of not word-one from *you.* That was really mean, Nick . . . But Mungo, at least he helped me. Bip certainly did. But not you."

His profile was stony. Forcing her to go further than she knew she should. "I wanted him, I had him, even if the man might as well not have been there when it happened, but it did happen, and it was fine, Nicky, and you'll just have to get used to it. A mistake, a fine fucking mistake."

A small muscle in his jaw began to twitch; the coarse skin jumped and rippled. To her silence he said nothing.

He finally turned his head to look down at her. As she pushed a stream of breath from her nostrils to keep herself steady, she believed him — eyes, mouth, skin — to be *him:* the basic Winnoe, all guises stripped away.

"You're right, Syl," he said, and before she could react to what she wanted to consider a clear recognition of their mutual guilt, he added, perversely, *"Te absolvum,"* and the words, when they came, were uttered in the sepulchral tones of a black priest.

"I don't want to be absolved, you asshole, I want you to love me." She was panting.

"I do," he said quickly.

"What?"

"Love you."

She gave way, seemed to be falling toward him, and as his huge hands reached out to catch her she saw that someone was running up the hill at them. Nick took her by one elbow, supported her, as he turned them both to face Oliver, who scrambled upwards in a spidery, fluid way that reminded Sylvia of Stanley. Oliver came to an abrupt halt in front of them.

"My mom says there's a phone call for one of you," he said.

"Thanks, kid," Nick growled; the bastard had slipped back into his public character like a pair of old Levis.

Oliver ran on to the house ahead of them, and she followed Nick to the porch and into the kitchen, feeling as if she could handle whatever string-pulling would now take place. At least something true had happened on the hill, no matter how momentary. She knew the phone could only mean instructions for survival, and she hoped the hell movement would result, but when Nick went into the living room to the phone, Sara came from there, and Sylvia's insides went weak, slushy.

"Are you all right?" Sara asked, lightly touching the material of Sylvia's T-shirt in a gesture charged enough with affection or concern or love that Sylvia felt a near-painful heat on her skin beneath the cotton. These small, emotional winds would wreck her yet, she thought.

She sighed, struggling for control. "It's my period," she said. She heard Nick's voice, low and rasping, indistinct.

"Maybe you'd like to take a bath," Sara offered, removing her hand. "Use the bathroom upstairs."

"Oh, would I."

Sylvia retrieved her bag from the porch and, passing Sara,

entered into the living room, where Nick winked at her as she climbed the stairs. She walked along the balcony, found the bathroom, and while she put in a new tampon listened to the welcome flow of hot water.

After taking off the stained clothes she eased her way into the tub, until finally she was submerged but for her nipples, the ridge of scar, and a bubbly curl of pubic hair. She drifted and faded in an envelope of heat and water and over-bright images that went flowing through her brain unbeckoned, fragmentary, comfortable: the double-jointed thumb of a younger Nick Winnoe; a swatch of cheap government-green curtain stirring in the Santa Ana; sparks from a steel comb passing through Bip's hair; a drop of sea water like sperm on Croquet's ivory breast; and Sara's fine-boned hand floating in emerald space, gesturing forcefully . . . and — then — nothing. . .

Until she opened her eyes to find Nick gazing down upon her with an expression that seemed to her to mix equal parts of passion and guile.

"You know," he said, "I'd almost forgotten the scar."

"Some memory," she said lazily, and watched him as he went down on his knees beside the tub and kissed over her belly several slow times. "Who was on the phone?" she asked when he began to move his face toward her breasts.

He kissed again. "Othello, my dear Des. He and another black person, a friend of yours, are on their way."

Sylvia lifted her head from the slope of the tub and grabbed Nick's ears to make him stop his business.

"On their way here? That's wonderful."

"Umm. He's gonna put us all on a spacecraft. But Iago remains at large."

"If you mean Stanley," she said, "he'll come up here if he knows that's where Bip is."

"The last thing we need is a cokehead," Nick said, falling back on his heels and looking, for a moment, more somber than she knew he'd meant to. "Come on, let's go get a room at the Inn and fornicate until time and the others catch up with us. Othello is also bringing his personal photographer."

"Don't you have a home?" she asked, feeling stupid for

not knowing.

"Yes, but prudence—"

"Yeah, yeah. Listen, will you ask Sara to loan me some clothes. I've been wearing other people's since Bip destroyed mine. Might as well have one more set, then *you* can buy me some new."

He smiled broadly. "What do you want?"

She told him that pants and some sort of shirt would do; she'd stay with Croquet's windbreaker and the smelly boots. Nick left. She dried herself, and after a while he returned with an outfit that was large but suitable; the white chambray shirt smelled of lilacs.

Nick had left her while she dressed, and when she emerged from the bathroom onto the balcony she saw that below her the living room was empty, though she could hear voices from the kitchen. She moved the length of the balcony, and as she was descending the stairs was startled to see the figure of a man standing in the alcove. His round, muscular back was toward her and he seemed to be swaying clumsily to a music only he could hear. When he heard her descent he turned, stooped and still rocking in place ... like a lowering and wary black bear Sylvia had once seen in the San Diego Zoo.

CHAPTER EIGHT

Gonna get me a flute and a gun that shoots.

New England
May 2, 1970

BLOUNT, you'll recall, had earlier fled to the isolated and
possibly purifying chamber of his workroom, where his few
pages of manuscript lay derisively alongside his typewriter. He
had sat down, the sweat from his aborted game with Oliver
cooling slowly, and typed off in furious succession several
pages of (he thought) advancing story and fairly limber tone,
finally completing the passage begun so far away in time —
my god, yesterday — that he had to struggle to recall what he
had been thinking when he wrote:

> *I've never told you this, but she had to taste*
> *herself before she could come. Yes, one taste*
> *and she'd be gone. There was nothing ambig-*
> *uous about her, no; my wife was more or less*
> *a complete lie. Her other lunacies surrounded*
> *me like puling kittens. She read Anaïs Nin, all*

123

of it, and went around saying, "I have to dis-
cover my lesbian self." I couldn't stand it,
the foolishness of her horrible declaration.
Where would she meet that self? In secret
societies? Art galleries? A church? That was
it! She'd taken her first screwing from a
Catholic priest in a thunderstorm on Long
Island Sound, and now she would get even
with Holy Mother Church once and for all.
This was my wife! Finally, I had to follow
her, skulk after her wherever she went . . .

But soon enough the welcome tunnel-vision had closed over his brain like a cowl, and he was able to maintain at a great distance the snarls and barks of the world outside.

At an earlier time [he continued, later in the narrative] *we both took as lovers a couple called Hansen — you remember, the man with the cruel mouth, and his hobbledehoy wife, the short one who thought so much she developed paralysis of the brain — and on Christmas Eve of 1968, with the War waging only a television away, we four gathered ourselves before my fireplace, on my mohair rug spread over with two thin pallets, and drank my fine cognac in excessive amounts until we were all befogged into that unreal equality that comes with such drinking; we became the sort of opiated group that drives me as silent as foam, though my wife it stimulates to a controlled frenzy of sensual gobbling. I know you remember that ever-sampling forefinger of hers . . . I know you've licked that finger yourself. But it's the Hansens that I remember now, those hoarders of jealousy and spite. Near midnight, after Mrs. Hansen had blown out all but one candle and passed a joint that all but I partook of, I discovered that a mute mitosis had taken place, that Mrs. Hansen was prone with me on one pallet, that Hansen himself was being expertly kissed by my own wife, as if he were a mound of truffles, on the other. Yet we were all as close and as cozy as nursing shoats. I knew Mrs. Hansen would not act, but*

*would receive, and so I undertook to kiss her . . . the next
thing being evident to me was that we had become heaps
of flesh, copulating like Bosch midgets, my mind said as it
rose to the ceiling omnisciently, only to be brought down
by the hairy knuckles of Hansen caressing my own palm
in the accidental jostle of all of our coupling. Convulsively I
flicked my hand and felt him jerk away, surely every bit as
repulsed as I. The women continued unaware. Mrs. Hansen,
under me, had furrowed her forehead like a child concentrat-
ing on her math homework, and I knew that shortly she
would release her breath and give up, privately telling herself
she didn't deserve the tender spasm anyway. I released my
sperm into her without a sign. She did release her breath. We
lay among each other long enough for the sounds of the other
two to become clear. Out of the corner of my eye I saw that
my wife was very much on top of Hansen, that he was clutch-
ing desperately to her neck, while she went at him, perpetual
and greedy. But you and I know she cannot make it without
that taste of herself, which I doubted Hansen had given her.
Just then, Mrs. Hansen, in the embarrassed stews of herself,
said something silly like, "Hey, quit rockin' the boat," which
was enough to bring the other couple to an abrupt halt. We
all rolled sideways to one another and pretended to great bliss
by means of sighs and other devices. At some point I rose for
more cognac, and when I returned to the scene my wife was
kneeling between the knees of Mrs. Hansen and about to
swoop into her groin. My brain screamed NO, but I maintained
enough aplomb to recline on one pallet, Hansen on the oppo-
site side of the two women, both of us as lazily observant as
life guards. The bitch buried her face in Mrs. Hansen, buried
and burrowed. One of her long thin hands crept up Mrs.
Hansen's torso and expertly tweaked one of the latter's soft
pink nipples. I shuddered. Here was that "lesbian self" de-
veloping right before my eyes, and not a blessed thing I could
do about it. What would follow seemed as clear to me as if I
had a booklet and diagrams; sure enough, after their breathing
had increased in a bewildering way, they reversed roles, and
now Mrs. Hansen did the honors while my wife lay on her*

back, spreadeagled, with virtually her entire fist crammed into her own mouth. Events speeded. She reached down for Mrs. Hansen, and as she drew her up she rolled them both over, so that by the time I could see again she was lapping at Mrs. Hansen's mouth (that taste!) and grinding her pelvis, uttering small screams that rose in pitch until I saw her shoulders suddenly release to limpness, and in the silence I could see Mrs. Hansen's brow, still furrowed, and I knew that only my wife and I had gotten our rocks off this time around. Tough for the Hansens. But one more blow at Holy Mother Church for my wife . . .

Here, Blount lost his way, lost the thread, lost the vague erection that pulsed against his jock strap, and felt cold and disgusted; he became aware of the silence, of the empty house behind him, of the window before him through which he could see mocking fields of rock and spring greenery. He decided to go and change his clothes, perhaps drink a beer and wander outside and attempt conversation with his family. The tiredness in his bones and muscles would soon enough disappear; the week-end would end quietly, lazily; surely it would.

But when he reached the living room he saw out of the window, on the wide lawn, glowing in the soft late light, cross-legged together on the grass, his wife, youngest son, and a woman. A woman he knew immediately to be Sylvia Winnoe; her hair shone unnaturally golden and her hands were gesturing in slow, gentle motion. He wanted more, wanted to be closer to both of the women. But without actually going there and involving the risky possibilities of speech. He backed up to the record player alcove and picked up a pair of dusty binoculars which he cleaned with the tail of his shirt as he stepped back to the window. He adjusted the focus until it became hard and clear before him: Sylvia's ear in focus; Sylvia's childish pallor; her thin blue shirt hanging loose from her shoulders; and Sylvia's hands moving to her breast as she (apparently) listened to the words that flowed with silent exuberance from Sara's mouth. What could Sylvia be hearing? Was this convict, this tacky but beautiful fugitive, now receiving some easy rhetoric of instant conversion? Blount knew a

curious sympathy — as if he had suddenly assumed the pro-
tection of Sylvia Winnoe and must stand stalwartly between
her and such artful bamboozlers as Sara, or Nick Winnoe. But
before he could go further with this, another voice broke in:
you're a jerk, he told himself, lowering the glasses.

He walked into the bedroom and yanked off his shirt and
shorts and jock; stood nude in the center of the room trying
to determine whether or not to shower the dried sweat from
his body. Yes, he would; he'd try the sluicing trick, and per-
haps he could get back on the private track he had lost — it
now seemed — the day Monica had walked into his house.
Damn women!

In the shower he was bemused to discover his mind play-
ing pleasant tricks on him; his memory rather than his present-
tense voice was in the process of taking charge, and a wet day-
dream of Sara began to flow; a montage that was fleshy, yes,
but also kind and funny and not without, he realized as it was
going on, a certain amount of ordinary nostalgia for their days
in Cambridge, 1963, where they had met in the first place. He
remembered weighing 145 pounds. It was June. The room-
mate did something; he came in — Tim something — and said
to Blount: "Do you think it's all right to plank my cousin?"
When Blount shrugged, Tim blushed, picked his nose, and
told him in a stuttering rush that his cousin, Sara Leary, would
arrive from Bridgeport that afternoon and he didn't want any-
thing to do with her, or any other woman for that matter.
Blount sympathized. He weighed 145 pounds and felt light-
headed most of the time; the girl he had in Maine thought he
was "inner-directed and selfish." He asked Tim what this
cousin wanted. Tim only knew that she was coming there to
school, that he was supposed to help her out, somehow. Blount
looked at him for a while and then said he'd take care of it.
Tim was relieved. He left Blount alone in the apartment.

Sara walked in. And that was it. Details didn't matter;
her mouth took his heart and poked it; her size made him
tremble, even more lightheaded. "I'm going to Myrtle Beach,"
she announced brightly, "and I'd appreciate it if you'd have
Tim cover for me while I'm gone. He can tell my mother and

dad I'm out looking for a job." Blount had made her delay her departure by two hours, and now — in the shower — he watched her across from him in the Greek restaurant as she carefully cut her souvlaka and told him she'd never settle for less than the best. She left. He passed the summer, or some part of it; the girl in Maine came down with a case of shellfish poisoning. One day in August, long after Tim had had to tell Bridgeport that he knew not where his cousin was, she returned on the back of a huge black motorcycle driven by a hairy person named Jack. Blount could see it, palpable: the cycle at the curb; the breezy, long-legged girl unpinning her haversack from the other junk; the disdainful Jack enshrined in a yellow helmet all dented and pocked; the feeling in Blount's heart that something large would occur if he only stayed on the sidewalk and waited for Sara to speak. Which she did. "I owe this man $35 for the trip. Would you please pay him."

Something large. He only *had* a little more than a hundred dollars, but he went upstairs and got the fare. Jack shook his head and drove off, free. Sara had never said another word about this transaction. And neither had Blount.

He turned off the shower and dried himself. Was Sylvia's arrival also something "large"? Something he would gladly pay for? He wanted to think not; but inside him her tense pallor pulled strings of contradiction he barely understood: she reeked of crime and death and the possibility of harming others, yet through the binoculars she had seemed as beautiful and frail as Sara was beautiful and tough.

In the bedroom, dressing, he resumed cussing himself . . . but now it was for the romantic flatulence of the shower. He'd return to work soon, return to his real business, which surely meant more than any historical Cambridge idyll. However, as he buttoned his shirt, a whining tapping vehicle came up the driveway, and he glanced out the window and saw, with a groan, that it was Nick Winnoe returned to claim his long-lost mate. Fuck these people!

He met Nick in the kitchen. The man was breathing through his mouth, almost snorting as he stared out the window at the women in the backyard.

"She's here, huh," Nick said; he did not look at Blount.

"It seems so."

"Christ, what's she done with her hair?" Nick whispered.

"Pardon?" Nick looked at him impatiently.

"I said, how are you. You calmed down?" But you could see his concentration changing gears.

"Of course. What are your plans?" Blount asked evenly.

Nick wrinkled his porous nose and fiddled with the sink faucet with his right hand; water dribbled in the silence.

"I don't know," he said. "I'm expecting a phone call."

"Here?" Blount said.

"Your number's in the book."

"Perhaps the FBI already has it," Blount said, with heavy sarcasm.

"Look, Christopher, just relax, will you. Everything's going to be okay if all the good people will stay cool. I'm going out to see my wife now, with your permission."

Blount recognized the real anxiety in the other man, but couldn't resist another question. "Then what?"

Nick barked his laugh. "Then, as they used to say, passion will rear its head," he said. "Unless she's been pulling that albino joker's joint." He smiled grimly and turned his head back to the window. "Or the cokehead's."

"You're mumbling, Nick," Blount said.

"No sir, I'm not doing that, I have to get up my nerve to go out there, you know. It takes time. Listen, we-I may ask you a favor."

"I'm already doing you a favor," Blount said.

"I know, I know, I appreciate it, but this is something *more*. Come'ere." He seized Blount's shoulder and pulled him, against his resistance, toward the window. "Now look; you wouldn't want to see that piece of cake busted, would you? Two years is bad enough. Am I right?"

Nick's meaty hand rested on his shoulder as light as a mitten.

"Yes," said Blount.

"Yes is right. So, stand by. Just a bit of driving. It looks like Sara won't have any objections, either."

And with a squeeze for Blount's shoulder, Nick left. His heat remained on his skin as he watched the man amble toward the two women, watched the embrace, and then Sara was coming along to the house in a way so confident that he felt a reflexive unwillingness to speak with her — some quirk to do with his memories in the shower, as if he wanted to stick with the motorcycle memory of the girl instead of this proud woman. He was back in the workroom before she could enter the kitchen.

Once there, he sat down in front of the typewriter and told himself he would pursue cold reason with a vengeance. On the paper in the machine he read: *But one more blow at Holy Mother Church for my wife;* and, askew on one corner of his table, the page that began, *I've never told you this but . . .*

He closed his eyes and groaned. Shit. Reason. Reasoning. This fiction was not reasoning; it was sublimation of the worst sort; it was a series of scornful little images strung together to make a lie; it was crueler to Sara and everything she *was* than if he had stood in rags on a street corner and sold her off piece by piece to passing cannibals. Why didn't he write about being light-headed in Cambridge? instead of about the made-up Hansens with their puerile, neurotic voluptuousness. He didn't know. What sort of distorting medium was he anyway? Monica had said he "giggled at history" in books that were "like beating off." Or had Pablo Eaton said that? Again, he groaned, and saw a flash of Sylvia's glowing hair behind his eyelids. Sara: "Chris, the women in this book are *bosoms;* they're unreal," she had said when he stood bleeding in front of her, almost killed by the man who now billed and cooed in his back yard.

Well, he could clean up this pottage of difficulties with a single stroke. He could enter into *real* and *normal* life with one healthy, socially responsible act. He would just flat call the authorities about the people in his yard who had ransacked his earned privacy. Why not? What a simple matter to pick up the telephone and say 'I know where you can find one of those people from the New York townhouse. Come fetch her from my property. I'm part of your system and I demand protection.' He heard the silence at the other end of the wire. Then: 'Would you repeat that please, Mr. Blount.' And the tape-recorders would whirr beyond his hearing.

Now he saw Sylvia slumped in a maroon cell, her hair dull with sweat and dirt. NO. No: unsatisfactory fantasy. Lousy notion. He would not be responsible for putting anyone in prison: evil institution. He wanted no such fate for Sylvia, for Nick, for any person. It would be as impossible for him to do this as to take his novel out of circulation, or prevent the publication of THINGS BURST, or stop writing . . .

He opened his eyes on the page in the typewriter: *Here was that "lesbian self" developing right before my eyes and not a damn thing I could do about it.*

Not so.

He ripped the page from the carriage.

Somewhere in the bowels of the house the phone rang several times, then stopped. The joker calling. Blount didn't care. He put the single page down on top of the others and rolled the whole manuscript into a tight cylinder that fit into his fist like a short bat. He searched over the table and in the shelves of junk found a book of matches. And, thinking Death to Anaïs Nin, Death to the Hansens, Death to Catholic priests, he went through the second door, which led to the garage. Outside, he walked past Winnoe's pickup and over to the rusted fifty-gallon drum he used to burn trash. In it he burned his pages, one by one; he let the process take its own slow, smoky time. Into domestic history, he thought glumly and with a certain lachrymose self-consciousness, and not one goddamn giggle.

Oliver stood beside him at the warm drum, had come up as silently as a cat.

"Dad."

Blount ran his fingers gladly up the back of Oliver's neck. "You scared me," he said.

Oliver looked pleased. "Are you finished working?"

"Yep."

"Can we play some ball?"

"It's getting late."

"Come on."

Blount watched the last page curl into blackness. "All right," he said, "for a little."

They went through the porch, catching sight of Sara at work in the kitchen, with Tom on a highchair nearby, and outside again, where they tossed the soft ball back and forth while the sun fell behind Dummer's Hill.

Blount felt relaxed if fragile, as though a hangover were just about to disappear forever. Nick came out of the house and joined the game. Clearly, for him, it was a most ordinary thing to do, but for Blount the arrival of the other man defined a mood he had barely been aware of; his anger at the simple act amazed him because he knew very well how childish it was. The next time the ball came his way he flung it towards the back field and watched Oliver hustle after it. "Shit, Daddy!" he yelled. Then Blount walked to the house, aware of Nick's wise smirk, and, once inside, stalked past Sara's turned back and into the living room, where he flicked on the record player without looking, and stood jiggling beside it while the nasal male voice crooned sorrowfully.

And, as you know, Sylvia came down the stairs. Her face appeared ghostly in the dim light, and she registered his presence only with a slight widening of her eyes. At the bottom of the stairs she stopped and faced him.

"Hello," she said, the syllables fast, deep like a man's. "I'm Sylvia Winnoe . . . but you ought to call me Margaret."

Blount smiled at her smile. Pleased with her honesty, which promised some perspective on the whole mess, he went towards her and stuck out his hand; hers came out and touched his. Like cool smooth sheets. Bloodless, he thought. He heard Sara come into the room behind him as he made this greeting to Sylvia, whose light brown eyes never left his face.

If this woman was in any pain she didn't show it.

The singing was cut-off in mid-phrase.

"You look so much better," Sara said to Sylvia. "The shirt's a bit big."

"I don't mind," Sylvia said. "It feels good."

She walked by Blount and he caught a scent of Sara, and something else . . . a vague sourness that was at the same time sweet, and fearful. She went to stand near Sara with her hands tucked away in the front pockets of the cord jeans; the green coat she'd had around her waist in the yard was now draped over her narrow shoulder. It must have been the coat that he smelled. Blount imagined an explosive powder invisibly coating the material. He saw the morning's news photo — the cylinders of water pouring into the steaming wreck.

"Would you like something to eat?" Sara was asking.

Sylvia shook her head. "No, thanks, you've done plenty. I think we should go."

Blount found himself crossing the room. "Go?" he blurted. He wanted to keep her — a wonderful and mysterious child come to visit, and not allowed to leave; Daddy Nick could go on down the road alone. Sylvia's quick smile seemed to take in and comprehend his rush of impossible feeling. It calmed him; he stopped and leaned his fingertips on the table.

"There's business to take care of," she said. "People. My friend Bip."

"You ought to get some sleep," Blount said gruffly.

"I'm sure I will, Chris," she said.

Sara laid a palm between Sylvia's shoulder blades. "I'm glad we got to talk. We'll see you again."

Sylvia nodded.

Then Nick barged in, heavy-footed and impatient. "Syl, come on." He glanced at Blount. "Before Christopher thinks up a good deed we might not appreciate."

The jibe embarrassed Blount. "Shoot," he said, trying to sound casual, deliberately drawling out the word.

"Anyway," Nick said, "we may be in touch." His glance was ponderous, sincere, knowing. "Don't worry, though. We're just going in pursuit of that passion I was telling you about. But don't *you* dwell on it." Unsubtle teasing, Blount thought.

"Fuck you, Jack," he said.

Nick laughed generously, but Sara frowned at Blount in a way she usually reserved for a child. Sylvia looked nothing if politely interested.

"You know," Nick said, "if you thought more of yourself, Blount, you'd be one hell of a guy." He turned to Sara and with elaborate politeness said, "Thanks for this; we won't forget it."

Nick reached for and clasped Sylvia's hand and they walked into the kitchen. Blount and Sara followed. Outside, in the twilight, Blount watched them climb into the pickup. As Nick backed the truck and turned he said something to Sylvia and she disappeared from the frame of windshield glass, vanished beneath the dashboard as if she had never been in the vehicle at all; and Nick was only driving off alone from a Saturday's neighborly visit.

Blount's argument with Sara after dinner was unexpected, quick and brutal. As he spun out of the driveway in the sedan, his headlights bouncing erratically over trees and shrubbery, he tried to face the fact that he was plain out of control of what he felt from moment to moment; or, as Sara had said at table, in reaction to his irritated remarks about the Winnoes, remarks made (he knew) only to cover over his affection for Sylvia, as well as his fear: "You could learn from women like Sylvia and Monica, Chris, believe me. They aren't so indrawn, so solipsistic; they don't confuse history and fantasy; they aren't unkind and suspicious and . . . so fucking nar-cis-sis-tic. They talk!" He had stood up, his jaw muscles pulsing like heartbeats, and walked straight from the house to the car, barely mindful that she near-shouted behind him: "That's right, leave. What you fear is words, you can't stomach *words* unless you're manipulating them. You know I'm right—" The door had slammed her silent.

But now, as he turned up the road to Bristol West, he damn well knew exactly what he was about. He believed Sara's eruption could only have been set off by her feelings for Monica; of course, he reasoned, Sara simply couldn't handle her two lovers equally, and Blount was receiving the raw end of the deal. Unfair, not just. And now that he had got shed of the Winnoes, and of his wretched pages, he could further clean house by taking care of Monica; he could forbid her to see Sara, and if she persisted he would tell her that he would take citizen's action against the whole bleeding lot of them. Surely she'd crumble before his threats. And while he was about it, he could seize Pablo Eaton and rub his face raw on the visible rocks of his property line . . . show the fucker that at least one novelist wasn't impotent and irresponsible. The *woulds* and *coulds* of his thinking surged unbeckoned in his shaky brain.

He leaned more toward the windshield, the road a bright grey smear before his squinting eyes; he had forgotten his night driving glasses. And his coat, too, he realized, trying to relax his shoulders and thigh muscles. He wanted a drink; wished himself sitting alone in some stark diner, at a long pearl counter, with a single dewy glass of beer in front of him like a magic totem as he sat with his back straight and a dove-colored fedora pulled low over his sorrowful eyes. Edward Hopper Blount, he said savagely to himself, downshifting for Dummer's Hill. This gauntlet of yammering had to stop, but it did not until he fishtailed the sedan up the Eaton driveway and came to a bucking halt.

When he emerged from the car he was struck for the third or fourth time by the soft yellow light that shone through the shaded windows of the house; but he shook off the forboding queerness of it and stamped to the side door. Raising his hand to knock he heard a sound in the barn behind him, a rapid scurrying, as if a large rodent had been disturbed at some project. Then there was a bang, a groan, a giggle, silence. Blount thumped harder on the door. He heard steps, the door opened, and he was admitted by Pablo Eaton.

"Hello," Pablo said, his surprise showing only in the deep furrowing of his forehead.

"Someone's in your barn," Blount said, walking past him and toward the light of the kitchen.

Pablo shut the door. "Really," he said matter-of-factly; it was not a question. "To what do we owe this visit?"

Blount halted in the kitchen doorway to allow his eyes to adjust to the light that came from a silvery kerosene lamp on the table. The amazing mess of the day before had disappeared, and at the dully glowing table sat Monica — demure, smiling, wearing a thick cable sweater — as if she had been waiting for him. Lucia Eaton was nowhere to be seen, but from another room he could hear an extremely vibrato woman's voice singing, "Ma said, Pa said we must keep on dancin'. . . "

Blount walked toward Monica on the balls of his feet, his lips pressed tightly together. He could feel Pablo behind him, halted in the doorway.

Monica erased her smile but casually indicated that Blount should have a seat next to her. He shook his head and stood looking down at her, rocking back and forth on his feet.

"Hi, Chris," she said finally, the disarming lilt, as always, there like a taunt.

"Can I offer you a drink?" Pablo asked.

"You better shoot the varmit in the barn first," Blount countered, though he was still looking at Monica.

"No sweat," Pablo said. "Come on, have a whiskey."

"No thanks."

Monica made a gesture with her thumb and forefinger. A flicking motion, he thought. And out of the corner of his eye he saw Pablo back through the door and close it. Then the outside door slammed.

"Please sit down," she said firmly. "I can imagine why you're here and I don't think you're gonna beat me up, so don't stand there looking so silly."

He sat.

His hands, curled into half-fists, lay on the table in front of him. He noted, as if they were not his, how much they resembled Nick's. Short and thick, like pickles. He slumped in the chair, allowed his chin to fall toward his chest while he waited to hear what he was going to say.

"Ma said, Pa said . . . " and the singing voice changed rapidly to a risque version of "Bye Bye, Blackbird."

Monica reached for a knob on the lamp and turned up the light until it nearly glared. Now Blount could see into the corners of the spotless room. The light prompted him to speak.

"I won't share my wife with you," he said, into the distance, to the blackness of the wood stove.

After a moment, Monica said softly, "I didn't know we were sharing."

He took a breath, another. A shape under the stove moved slightly; it was the rock-eating dog, he realized, like a dusty corpse. "Don't be naive," he said, closing his fists. She shifted in her chair. "Sara is just . . . experimenting with you; you're part of a test, a ploy to get at me."

Her hand entered into his sight and came to rest on one of his fists; it lay there like a fork made of soft putty.

"You don't believe that junk," she said easily. "If you'd quit talking with your balls you'd see a thing or two."

"Oh?" He moved his hand, displacing hers. "Such as?"

"I don't know; maybe that you aren't the only one with an imagination; that Sara can and will follow hers, her imagination, wherever's good. You can understand this, easy as pie." And she added, graciously enough to avoid whatever patronizing was taking place, "Your limits aren't her limits."

"Puerile chatter," Blount said slowly, knowing immediately that he did not mean it.

"Right, right. That's a good Blount phrase. I'm not out to hurt you. I love Sara and I could love you if you'd let go. Sara loves me, she loves you. Differently, but all love. You can bet your firehose on it."

"My what?" he asked stupidly. He felt a grief like a peaceful weight on his chest.

"Your cock, your thing that bursts so silently in the

dark of night."

He allowed his palm to flop on the surface of the table and she touched him again with two of her fingers. Outside a chicken squawked, and in the far room the woman's voice trailed off. He could actually see his next words forming in the front of his brain, in bold capital letters like a billboard far off from his moving self: ALL RIGHT, ALL RIGHT, PEACE ON EARTH, GOOD WILL TOWARDS WOMEN . . . but before he could offer these words of what he knew to be mildly honest relinquishment, in a form that would let Monica know that he had *heard,* the kitchen door was jerked open and into the room sprang a wiry little man, all kinetic and rubbery, with a head of startling red hair that was so shot through with spikes of hay that at first Blount throught he wore some grisly helmet of war. Blount was half out of his chair before he felt Monica's hand on his thigh, urging him to sit back down, almost forcing him with its hard grip.

The man had stopped in the center of the room, though his entire body, dressed in dark colors, seemed to ripple and tremble beneath the cloth. At his temple, Blount could see now, was a purpling splotch, nearly square. His mouth opened and closed several times, as though he were in desperate search of air or words; in fact, his nose wrinkled, unwrinkled convulsively. Twitches, tics, tremors. Of this rabbit Blount could not be afraid.

Pablo came into the doorway and stood casually, almost deferentially.

"This is Stanley from Hollywood," Pablo said, akin to introducing a brand new kid on the block.

The strange sound Blount heard, had been hearing, was Stanley's chattering teeth, like dice shaken in a leather cup.

"Stanley's strung out," Monica observed. "We found him stoned in the cemetery, didn't we, Stanley?"

A child's voice carried through the house. "Momma, don't!"

Apparently this cue set Stanley off; his face changed shape, became suddenly handsome, composed and reasonable, as though he had just conquered a horrible stage fright.

"And you are?" he said, looking straight at Blount for the first time.

Monica identified him.

"Ah!" Stanley sang, raising both of his hands, palms forward, to Blount. "Your work is known to us . . . to me." He bowed slightly, then fluttered his hands like fans. "The White House is ever grateful for men like you who while away their time in frivolous wordpeckering, if you get my meaning. In Ameri-ka, writers know their place; they know that the three greatest virtues are screwing, drinking and lying. Why, I once spent an hour alone in a kitchen with the fierce and famous Norman Mailer. But, oddly, I found him so kind, even meek, that I thought I was being stroked with a soft glove; nothing like marijuana to calm a public ogre, to reveal him as a puppy, as a precocious child who never wielded anything more dangerous than a pen knife, or a monomaniacal pen. Toys!"

"Stanley," Pablo tried to interrupt.

"What autoerotic scribbler in this country, this comfortable country, would dare pick up the gun? So, what we do, you see, is make it easier for 'em to stay seated at their fancy Selectrics; we give them MONEY, money for the ARTS; and after they've fed at the trough — that's good, good, I bumped my fucking head on one of your troughs, there, Pablo — once or twice, they're spoiled forever. Ha ha."

"Shut up, Stanley," Pablo said. "Blount isn't interested. If you don't stop gibbering, I'll start phoning for your buddy Silver."

A shadow of fright, no, concern, flitted over Stanley's face, sufficient to signal Blount that *somebody* had control over this sensible maniac.

Stanley crouched, curled his lip, and said, "I don't advise touching that telephone, Pablo baby. It might bite you." He straightened up and smiled, beautifully. "There's nothing worse than bodies that have been concussed by violent and immense explosions. The *flattening* is out-of-sight. Flat bones, man. It's very cold in here, you know. A little cold in the country." He groaned and clutched at his torso with his arms crossed over each other. "I'm sooo afraid of that Edmund

Silver. You know that feeling, Christopher? You ever been afraid of anybody? You ever had real power exercised over your self? Smug turd like you. You probably think I'm out of my gourd and therefore harmless as . . . " He came closer and put his smooth face near; Blount could see the fine texture of the almost-poreless flesh; the dog Jep rose unsteadily behind him. ". . . as that old dog over there. What do you say?"

Blount lifted his right hand from the table and placed the palm of it against the round of Stanley's chin. He then straightened his arm slowly against the resistance of that chin, and was pleased to watch Stanley tilted backwards and tripped up by the living carcass of the wandering dog, so that he (Stanley) fell flat to the floor and lay there with his arms spread out, laughing, while the dog turned and looked down at him with myopic curiosity.

Blount stood up and moved toward the fallen man, his hands curled low at his hips. This felt very good.

But Stanley just looked up at him and laughed and laughed. A perfectly sane laughter.

Monica had Blount by the elbow before he could decide what more to do with Stanley; as she had done before, she pressed his ulnar nerve and he found himself moving in the direction of the door. Pablo hung before him like a pudgy ornament. Blount attempted to glower at the man, but the pain at his elbow prevented this, and he exited with a mere nod, on a continuing wave of pain and Stanley's laughter.

When they were outside, Monica released him and then, curiously, put both of her arms around his neck and kissed him where his pocked cheek met his nose.

"Go home," she said, stepping back. "I'm sure Sara would rather have you there than here."

He touched the place she had kissed. "Who is that guy?"

"Oh, an old friend of Pablo's from the coast."

"Such friends," he said bleakly.

"It's okay, Chris. Nobody's after your ass. Go home to Sara."

He started at her indistinct face, could read only muted

solicitude.

"All right," he said finally, and turned to enter the sedan.

With the engine started, he turned on his headlights, and as he was backing around they caught not the image of Monica waving good-bye, but Stanley . . . now clad in a long navy watch coat, scampering from the door and into the dark of the barn. Blount flicked the beams up and down with his foot so that Stanley's run appeared in fast-motion, which struck Blount as a deliberate parody of a Charlie Chaplin anarchist fleeing the scene of his latest crime.

When he walked into his own kitchen he found it empty. The house was unnaturally silent until he came far enough into the living room to hear the quiet murmur of Sara's voice reading to the boys upstairs. He went back into the kitchen and fetched himself a glass of bourbon, which he drank slowly while sitting on the couch. He concentrated on his heartbeat, on the dull bang of the liquor as it worked in his stomach, and when he smoked a cigarette — his first since his drink with Sara the night before — a dizziness came over him strong enough to lay him back on the pillows. He flung the tube toward the cold fireplace. Still, the dizziness rang through his brain like hammer blows, and he believed for a moment that he would faint. He sat up quickly and put his head between his knees, taking gulps of chill air until things came right again, right enough for him to hear the tailend of the reading upstairs.

" . . . and into the village of Salem came a man with a face made of ice," she read, "and after he had done what he had to do to the family of Pitmans, the sun came out and melted him away to nothing but pure water. Nothing remained of him but a damp spot and the cloak of cerulean blue."

Her voice, which had grown louder as she came to the end, stopped.

After a silence, Oliver said, "That's funny, but I don't believe it for a minute. It's like one of Daddy's bedtime stories."

"No," said Sara slowly. "Not at all. Come on, get to bed now. Tom's already asleep."

"Yeah," Oliver said, "that book was too old for him."

Bedding down noises followed. Blount slowly recovered his proper metabolism. Sara came downstairs and sat beside him, quietly, as if nothing untoward had happened at dinner.

They watched his cigarette burn in the empty fireplace, both of them slumped against the pillows, as if, he thought, they had been watching a movie for too many hours. Sara signalled for the glass of bourbon he had retrieved from the floor and he gave it to her. She sipped, coughed lightly.

"I'm sorry," he said out of the blue, and although he meant the words, to him they sounded hollow and without meaning.

"No," she said quickly, "I'm sorry." Too quickly, perhaps, but he believed that the right signals had passed between them. She returned the glass and her hand fell to his thigh. "You must be tired," she offered. "You look awful. Where did you go?"

Without rancor he said, "Can't you guess?"

"Eatons'."

"Right." He took a good slow sip of the bourbon. "It was a matter of threatening Monica .. but naturally I couldn't."

Sara's hand tightened. "Why not?"

Blount sniffed and rubbed harshly at his nose. He doubted if he could give her a decent answer, but something must be said. "I guess I'm not much of a threatener," he said. "She's okay. Monica. And she does have a brain."

"Don't be smug."

"I'm *not*." Her hand moved, gentling him. "Look, it's simple: I'll be all right about you and her. I'll get used to it, Sara, but these other creeps are getting to me. It's too close to home. It's dangerous, and you know it."

Her sigh was like a pretty, nerve-wracking wind. "Can't you relax?" she asked.

"Just wait now." His voice was too sharp, and he brought

it as close to the matter-of-fact as he was able. "Out there at Pablo's I found some red-headed freak with a line of malarkey that didn't stop even when I knocked him on his rear. We don't have to have all these assholes crowding in on us, we just don't."

"I haven't met any assholes," she said quietly.

He counted to five and took another sip. "Go and meet this Stanley then."

Sara turned toward him and laid a cool hand across the back of his neck. "Why do you have to be so defensive? You could be a lot better at the unexpected . . . *we* could enjoy blesséd accidents, strange surprises, new tastes, people. We could."

"Yeah," he said, "it sounds like a plan for gourmet cannibals," but he had said it lightly, and she laughed a bit.

"I like Nick," she said, "and Sylvia even more. That's all that matters, love. We can lessen their trouble, and I don't believe it will cost us much at all."

"There's more to this than you know," he said, feeling pedantic and older than he wanted to admit.

"Bosh," said Sara, riffling his hair. "They just got caught playing games."

"Oh sure, games! People are dead, other people are running from the law; that's games? And they want us to help them!"

"But why not?" she said calmly. "The risks are so much smaller than what's to be gained by having Sylvia and her friend safely out of it."

At this he laughed; he gave up and laughed until even he could hear the echoes of Stanley in his unfettered noise. "All right, all right," he choked, "everything goes; we're free as fucking crows. No more judgments. Let it all happen, Sara my love."

She arranged for him a look that was at once haughty and sexual, then squeezed his neck until he had to flinch, but she smiled — apparently content to go along with the reckless mood into which he'd broken.

She took him to bed. Led him into the bedroom, undressed him, undressed herself — she did not ask him to shave — and they rolled themselves up onto the bed and lay side-by-side like old friends. He rested his left hand on her haunch, and with her head cradled in the crook of his right arm he could taste in her hair the soil and sun of her day — a good simple taste for Christopher Blount.

In a while she pulled the quilt over them, snuggled down on his chest, and settled her mouth on one of his nipples. Easy pressure, then a sharp needle dove in a bright line from his chest to the middle of his testicles. It was sufficient. It was unusual. And he liked it, and he knew she could tell. Her mouth came onto his, and it was soft and hungry. He responded in kind, his mind beginning to glow and go kaliedoscopic with a flutter of images that were in such close focus, and so brightly lit, that he could hardly identify them: the undercurve of Sara's left breast seen from below while she stood erect in the sunlight; Oliver's collar bone, as fragile as a twig covered with light chamois; the swatch of Sylvia's hair that rode just over her ear like a twist of molten wires; Monica's Adam's apple running a spectrum of colors, from indigo to apple red; a single pore on Nick Winnoe's nose, like a miniature bunker; and, that quickly, Blount had entered Sara, recognizing the familiar gasp, her knees adjusting themselves above his waist; this slow pleasure that so easily was forgotten in the light of day.

The tips of her fingers dottled his back and slid towards his buttocks; not urgent, not demanding, not anything but there. He stopped kissing her and buried his face in her neck, seeing — again — the pulses of image, completely unidentifiable now: shapes and textures, and the sound of the quilt, of her vulva, of the wind outside in the silver birch trees. This couldn't be right; too many procedures were missing, yet he was not able to concentrate on what they might be, and he barely stiffened, barely missed a beat, when she spoke aloud, spoke directly into his right ear. "I love you, Chris," she said. "I love what we do."

He accepted the words.

There was more, you could hear, but Blount had left his

mind, and when they came, not either one of them knew what noise they made.

Sometime later, both of them in half-sleep, she asked him to go and turn out the lights, lock the back door. He climbed down from the bed and put on her silky bathrobe; it felt fluid and luxurious on his skin. As he was about to shut the kitchen door and secure the lock, he decided to walk into the soft cool night and pee. Crossing the porch, he went out the driveway side and stood in the dirt behind the car, pissing in the moonlight.

The voice came from nowhere, to no one in particular it seemed, but it so frightened him that he jumped backwards and felt his urine splash his feet. From nowhere, it had said, "Love's quick pants." A deep resonant voice, yet whispering.

"Who is that?" he said, crouching and shaking his stained foot at the same time. He wanted a weapon, felt silly in the robe.

His night-vision came to him then. There was a figure leaning casually against the rear deck of the car. Blount walked closer, his calves tight, almost cramped. "Who is that? Stanley?"

Came a melodious chuckle and the gleam of teeth in a dark face, almost as if — he drew closer — the person were blacker than the night.

"I wanted to meet you, Mr. Blount."

"Don't tell me," Blount growled, now close enough to see that the man was black, had a high crest of afro, and was wearing a multi-colored vest that revealed a square of dark bosom. "Your name is Silver and you've come to make a fool of me." Adrenalin rang like music in his ears.

"Absolutely not," the man said, not moving a muscle; he could have been a queer tree, just delivered. "My name is Mungo Croquet."

"Lovely. I couldn't do better myself." Now Blount, too,

was whispering, the open bedroom window not fifteen feet away. "What do you want, now that you've met me?"

"I don't know."

"What!"

"Go back to bed," Croquet said. "Cleave yourself to that wonderful woman."

"Swine."

"O, o, o, I wouldn't say that." He made a dismissive gesture with one hand.

Blount used his fists to tighten the robe-sash around his waist. He didn't say anything: a waiting game for this unreal visitation.

Croquet's teeth glowed again and he reached a hand beneath his vest, seemed to scratch, then he yawned deeply and with apparent satisfaction, and began to walk bouncily away, passing close to Blount, who smelled witch hazel and oily make-up.

Blount said, "You're no black man."

But, you could hear, Croquet bopped on down the driveway without further comment.

Inside, Blount went about his domestic tasks, and when the house was dark, he re-entered the bedroom and easily fell asleep. The dream was brief, simple to remember: He was standing in the open portico of a great university's library; stretching out in front of him, as far as he could see, a sheet of white ice broken only in the far distance by needle-like vertical projections of black rock. He stood in the portico, confident, ready to begin some game without stakes, some contest to be approached with humor. A bell rang in the library behind him. The first shaft came arcing slowly through the air from the direction of the needles; it clattered on the marbled floor of the portico, a round-ended shaft, about six feet long, and made of a flexible blue-black metal. Several more of them missed him cleanly. But his time was coming; he knew it with an eager pleasure, and so the blow to his forehead, which was like being struck with a foam bat, caused him to cry out with joy. He picked up the shaft, bent and tied its business end into a knot, and, skipping toward the edge of the ice like a pole vaulter, hurled the shaft back. He saw it clear the needles and travel into the nothing.

CHAPTER NINE

I met one man who was wounded in love.

New England
May 3, 1970

CROQUET, midnight visitation in blackface, went walking rapidly along Blount's Silver Birch Road until he came to the rented automobile ("You and your wife have a real nice trip, Mr. Wicket," the woman at the counter had said, even in the face of Bip's scowl). He carried a preposterous and giddy sense of brotherhood with the weary man with whom he had just spoken, as well as a certain amusement at the way events were shaping . . . despite his discomfort at being in these sylvan country reaches, where even the peepers seemed to be speaking in tongues to him: messages of stillness and connected roots, of leaves moldering in the moonlight, that made Croquet long for a return to the quickened familiars of concrete and electricity and smudged glassy reflection.

He entered the sealed car where, to his relief, he could smell something of Bip's sweat, of Gjertrud's superior camera equipment, and a faint whiff of the oil that was the essense of the stain he had spread over his face, neck, chest, backs of hands, shins and calves. The flowering wig brushed the ceiling of the car as he fumbled for the keys, and found WABC New York in the leaping nighttime airwaves. Good enough! Cousin Brucie, speak to me now. Croquet hummed and heckled at the radio while he let the car roll silently down the hill — it wouldn't do to have Blount think he had come on other than raven's wings. At the hillbottom he fired the engine and swooped off in the direction Nick Winnoe had said would lead him to the wooden castle of Eaton.

The sealbeams buffeted the ancient trees as he sang at speed along the road's way, the City screaming at him, from the radio speakers: *NEWSTIME Newstime Newstime, You dig that in Cambodia, Cam-BOD-ia, ladies and chicks and guys and gents, you fasten on those BOMBS, do you, do you??? How 'bout that Mayor Lindsay, got booed in Queens once a-gain, can you dig it, That's our Mayor!*

O, it was gay and hopeless, and he flew on, beating his hand on the steering wheel in radio time: *That bombing, that bombing, that bombing . . . Village Bomb Factory bombed, kiddies! Little rich girl sought, and her NAKED companion . . . SDS denies all complicity . . . SDS is dead dead dead . . . as we leap right along ha ha ha to Bobby Dylan and "Subterranean Homesick BLUES," get it, you bet your WABC, 980 on the dial, 63 tragic degrees at 12-0-12, the RIGHT TIME for Cousin Brucie to duck out here for a PASTRAMI sandwich, WHEEE . . . .*

Some furry creature scurried into the headlights, something grey and piggish; he swerved to avoid the possum. But too late. The wheel went thump . . . thump. Damn. All things must live. Sad Possum Killer A'Loose in NEW ENGLAND.

Gay and hopeless. He came to the collection of square buildings he had been warned about, managed to find the right turning, and crept up the hill to Eatons'. Will these people be awake? He saw no light, not a one. No, not true, one upstairs, a corner window. He doused the car and, climbing out, slammed the door so hard the stars shimmied above his inflated head.

Waiting in the silence, his receptors tuned but producing

nothing but a vacuum of no-color, no-shape, he smelled, first, a sweet dust of manure and straw, then behind it an ancient wetness of swamp algae and mulch, and even beyond this was the cool smell of mica or slate or granite.

Stanley shouldn't be far off.

If only Decatur could be here to witness the coming masque, he thought; the capture of their elusive quarry in a silvery butterfly net. But someone *actual* was coming, now: a light blonde head floated against the greyish background of the doorway; in the foreground was a large animal the color of old leaves. Croquet moved past his automobile in the direction of the shadowed doorway. It was not a person he knew in the flesh, and thus must be Pablo Eaton . . . was Pablo Eaton who drifted through the door naked, preceded by what-was-now a dog, a dog with a purple nimbus of an idiot savant; behind it the pale flabby elongation of Eaton, with a member on him like a saint's lance. Sweet Hecuba, Croquet thought, what have we here?

In his brain's ear he heard the slow, rich click of a Nikon being fired. Yes, here was the photographer who was in love with Death.

"Pablo, baby," he said, street whispering, easy jive. "How they hangin'?"

"Silver, is that you?"

The dog waggled his head as if trying to think.

"Who else, brother? Mungo to you."

Croquet moved close enough to Pablo to put out his hand, palm up. Pablo brought his own arm up, and down in a slow arc that ended with a lazy slap which barely grazed the tips of Croquet's fingers.

"Nice to meet you," Pablo murmured. "Come in, I'm freezing my nuts."

The dog shambled away into the darkness and Croquet followed the fallen white globes of Pablo's ass into the black kitchen.

"No need to turn on the light," Croquet said. "I won't be long."

"I'll just poke up this fire," said Pablo, and after he spoke there was a clink of iron and a round of embrous light appeared beneath his hand. When Pablo leaned into the light with a short poker in his hand, Croquet could see clearly his orange and placid face. Behind the thin layer of illuminated skin was the skull of a grinning cadaver. Even Croquet shuddered at this morbid and false intimation as, you could see, he went rapidly into his detective act.

"Where's Stanley?"

About to replace the stovelid, Pablo turned his face and smiled; then the room, with another clink, went dark. "I don't know . . . but Jep out there ought to; the dog has a feel for certain things."

"Like what?"

"People about to run amok. Ask Chris Blount about Stanley. They had a little run-in earlier."

"Yes, yes," Croquet said aloud. COME ON, DONKEY-DICK, DON'T BE OBTUSE.

"Just follow the dog," Pablo said, with humor in his voice. "I'm guessing Stanley is somewhere in the woods talking to himself."

Croquet whistled under his breath. "Then we'll let *Jep* keep track of him; I'm not flitting around in the dark."

Pablo laughed. "Oh? Why not?"

"I've got to go," Croquet said. "I'll be back. Everything seems perfectly all right."

Pablo's silent derision came at him like a squiggle of brilliant neon; the source of this rudeness was beyond Croquet.

"Don't count on it," Eaton said.

Croquet gazed at the sepulchral shape of the other man. "We're all down at the Inn near the main highway. You care to join us? Stanley's Bip is there and she's anxious to know where he is."

Kitchen floorboards creaked. "No thanks. Lucia and I have better things to do, but you all might as well come up here tomorrow for something to eat. Catch Stanley in the daylight."

"By all means," said Croquet. "Sorry to disturb you. I can find my own way out. You've been very kind." Deliberate unctuousness on Croquet's part.

There was another short laugh, like a belch. "My pleasure, Mungo. You are one weird-looking person. Be careful."

"And may the world spare you also, sir. Hasta mañana."

Thus Croquet took his leave.

When he was again in the car he encountered a new smell, a dilution of damp wool and senile dog. Still, he cranked up, turned the radio louder, and backed his way around and out of the driveway. After covering a good mile, at speed, he flicked off the radio and said, "Stanley, you've sunk to a low state. What do you mean skulking around like this? You weren't meant for running in the woods, a man with your talents, your connections."

His speech brought no response. At the next curve he put the car into a four-wheel drift and was pleased to come out of it just as the vehicle passed over a hump of frost heave that sent it briefly into the air, and then down hard on the shocks.

A satisfying grunt from his stowaway.

TALK, SPIDER.

"Stanley," Croquet said with mock gravity, "you're not yourself. You must have something to say or you wouldn't be here. I've missed your talkative presence since . . . ahh, Friday afternoon. I had to come all the way to this backwater to find your double-dealing ass."

A head rose into the rearview. "I beg your pardon," it said angrily, and Croquet smelled a breath of gin and old liverwurst.

"If you've turned into a gunsel and are about to stick your piece in my ear, I want you to understand that I'll jerk this steering wheel much too sharply to the left, and we happen to be going fifty-eight miles per hour." Spoken sonorously.

"I never owned a gun in my life, Silver, and you know it. I use my head."

"Cool it, I'm only checking up on you."

"You needn't. Jesus, what've you done to your face?" Stanley asked, peering.

"Bip and I decided that an interracial couple departing New York City on this particular week-end wasn't prudent. The fact that we had to bring Gjertrud, who is white, was definitely a crack in the façade, but we seem to have made it."

"Bip?" Stanley was no longer feigning a lack of words; the concern read genuine.

"You thought she maybe died, got blown away?"

"No," he said quickly. "I knew that didn't happen. I read the newspaper. I thought—"

"You canny bastard, I know what you thought!" Croquet came onto the flat and increased his speed. "You thought I'd send her back to California, out of harm's way so you could work your schemes without having to worry about *her.*"

Stanley reached a hand over the seat and tapped a finger three times on Croquet's vested shoulder; they were not kind taps.

"Listen," he said in his most rapid voice, "when you sent Decatur after me I knew you'd sprung a lobe. You made a mistake not trusting me; I had nothing at all to do with Sylvia and Bip being busted at that demonstration; I don't fuck with the Special Tac people and you know it . . . but what did happen to me Friday was that I was accosted on the street, on my way to see *you,* by the same undercover Federal narc who set me up two Christmases ago, when Bip took the rap and went in. This geek laid a threat on me I could not ignore."

"Did he now?" Croquet said, slowing the car.

"Listen to me, dammit! This man — his name is Freddie Bartholomex — said that Liebling, the one that Bip and Sylvia delivered the coke to, had named ME as his principal connection, had told him I was the fucking King of the Hollywood snow merchants, and that if I didn't co-operate right then and there, he'd have me in the can before I could catch my breath."

They passed the turn-off to Blount's house. Croquet did not at all want to believe this tale of Stanley's, though he did sense truth radiating from the back seat like body odor. "So you did what, co-operated how?" Croquet asked.

Stanley sneezed, then giggled like an automatic weapon being fired in quick-burst.

"Freddie B. gives me all these phone numbers and says to keep in touch no matter where I am, and then he goes so far as to inform me that I'd get *fees*, like bounties, for every serious leftie — your doctrinaire bombers and so forth — I fingered."

Clumps of light shone ahead of them; Croquet scratched nervously at his stained chest. "Cock and bull," he muttered.

"Yeah, well, maybe so, but sharp Freddie knew exactly where Sylvia stayed when she came out of Terminal Island, and you know he knows Bip, and I swear to you, Silver-fish, he asked if I were by any chance in New York to see some of my friends in the *theatre* world."

"O swell." Croquet's throat tasted of dust and mendacity. The village of Windsor rose below them, shoddy buildings scattered willy-nilly along the roadway. "I tell you, Stanley, Bip will be all right, Sylvia too. You'll see soon enough, and the rest of it will be over before the sun sets on Eaton's swamp Sunday night."

"Such confidence; it's fuckin' bravado is what it is."

"Look," Croquet hurried to say, "we can always move north for a rendezvous in Montreal with that Quebeccer saint I've told you about. We'll call Freddie from there."

"Come off it, Silver, I'm not one of your devotees."

At the stop sign in the center of the village Croquet carefully came to a complete stop, and as he did Stanley pushed forward the passenger seat, reached for the door handle, opened the door, and in a flash of dark great coat negotiated himself into the front seat; they moved on through the sign and along the main road to the freeway that did, in fact, lead north to Montreal.

Stanley's relocation seemed to produce a subtle transformation in the man; he beat one set of fingers on the dash in a rhythm both dissonant and quickening. The small, carrot-topped figure bent toward the windshield, tapping away, as if he were a child eager to reach an amusement park the likes of which he had never seen but had heard of in vivid detail. Croquet drove the speed-limit and attempted to read this new mood in his compatriot. Stanley leaned back in the seat and reached into the front of his coat, searched briefly, and then pulled forth a small twist of silken material that glowed pearl in the dash lights. He put two fingers into the poke, as if dipping snuff, and then, indeed, the two compressed fingers darted for his nose and there followed a sniff, dip again, a stronger sniff like a grampus with catarrh.

"So," Croquet said, "I've been talking with a deprived coke fiend."

"Balls," Stanley sighed, sitting up in the seat. "Just straightening out for the strenuous times to come. I want to be at my best, not only with sweet Bip . . . but with Sylvia, who kissed me."

"Her husband Nick is down here at the Inn."

"Big deal, beezelbub. I know you put your icy prong in her; you couldn't resist. And don't think Nick isn't ready to murder you. Mark my words. What a bunch you've got, Mr. Silver!"

"You never know when to stop, do you?"

"You've been warned," Stanley crowed. "I'll now retreat into my private fantasies of wealth and high position, where bellicose writers and fartsie magicians and sad ladies are all kept baying in locked dungeons while I spend all my time on the telephone to the likes of J. Paul Getty, the poor Hunts, and even Henry Ford, who just last month had me stuff the lining of his Dop Kit with a substance so pure you could still smell the splayed feet of the Colombians."

"There you go again," Croquet said, relieved to spot the red neon sign of the Windsor Inn in the distance. "I hope Bip will take you off and vacuum out your head."

Croquet wheeled the car onto the pea gravel and drove slowly past the office and the cars parked in front of the Inn's bar, from which he could sense, even through the closed windows of both car and building, the monotonous thumping of a live bass guitar. He brought the car to a halt at the far end of the separate motel building, next to Nick's pickup, and before they got out he told Stanley that he would find Bip asleep in Room #8 — he handed him the key — that he would be in #7 with Gjertrud; and the Winnoes in #6 . . . all of these connected by an outside balcony that ran the length of the second floor of the building. Stanley produced a confident laugh and popped from the car while Croquet silenced the engine and moved himself to join this chain of fortunate couples.

He inserted the key in the lock of #7, and as the door swung open on the darkened interior, he heard a rustle, a series of metallic clicks, and suddenly a strobe light set in the low ranges began to pulse bluely into his eyes. Behind the source of the intermittent light, snapping away with her camera, was Gjertrud, although he could see her only as a shape, elbows spread in order to work the machinery that was freezing him again and again. Croquet turned stately; he walked forward into the room, twisting his head this way and that, so she would have every opportunity to capture the contradictions of his profile. Half-way across the room he reached up and drew from his head the afro wig, and it was this photograph — the walnut skin, the white teeth smiling, and the crown of his own ice-colored hair, curved and flattened by the wig — that he knew Gjertrud would save until the day she died: her previous Tommy, half-in, half-out of himself.

And, indeed, although the strobe kept up its singing electronic pulses of cold light, she had stopped working the camera, and was laughing softly behind all the paraphernalia. No matter how unwise all this was, this recording of the visible, Croquet knew he had to indulge her imagination in order to keep the peace, at least in room #7.

"The midnight rambler returns," she said, speeding up the strobe. It seemed to him they were standing inside of a television's tube. "While you were out I prepared myself with unguents and oils, and found this lovely caftan in your bag..." She whirled about, the strobe light on its straps at her waist sending waves through the room; the camera slung around her neck rose from her chest and the skirt of the garment formed like a bell around her legs. " . . . you owe me *something* for all this travel and waiting about, and the fact that I'm scared."

"Turn it off," he said.

The room went from blue to grey to black; he saw her after-image as it began to move for the bed, working the various leather straps over her head. Then the vague bedside lamp came on and she was standing beside it simply — a girl in her nightgown. Watching him.

He took off the vest and dropped it to the floor. Dropped the black trousers, kicked off the soft slippers, and was naked before her. She put one hand over her mouth as if to suppress minor amusement.

"Come," he said, "help me get this stuff off." He moved to the vanity table and sat down in front of the mirror. She came up behind him and touched his shoulder blades.

"No wings," she said. "Real flesh. Tommy Wicket down to the bare essentials." Her hand traced his backbone down to the coccyx, then slid upwards again. Goosebumps rose on his thighs.

"Gjertrud," he said slowly.

"Sir."

He picked up a small bottle of clear liquid from the surface in front of him and handed it back over his shoulder. A tissue from the box followed. "Clean my face and the rest."

She used the sharp-smelling acetone deftly, until his face was clear, unstained; then she moved down his throat and neck, over his chest, and finally knelt at his feet until the area from knees to ankles was as white as milk. When she had finished they both stood up and she wrinkled her nose at the chemical smell that saturated the air around them. He led her into the bathroom, turned on the shower, removed the caftan from her body, and they stepped together into the hot water, where he purified the chemistry, and afterwards made love to her standing up, his fists on a towel rack, until they both fell sideways against the tiles of the wall.

Back from the dead, she winked at him, turned off the water, and stepped out onto the mat. He watched her slowly dry herself, watched her relaxed but thoughtful face, and when

157

she was finished, she said, as though she had discovered some useful truth, "This is real sperm leaking out of me, Tommy. You're an imposter." She rolled her towel into a loose cylinder and popped it at his genitals. Missed. But she laughed anyway, turned her small ass on him and left the bathroom humming a tune.

They eventually went to bed and slept like elegant mummies through the rest of the night.

Mid-morning Croquet arose, and while Gjertrud slept on he prepared himself for the day ahead. He went into the bathroom and shaved his face. Then, using a pair of scissors and his straight razor, he removed every trace of hair on his head. His final pleasure was to pat the entire shiny surface with a measure of witch hazel, from Adam's apple to crown to occiput. As his pate sang and stung he stood quite still and observed in the mirror his stripped self: a blanched Goya nobleman, with pinked eyes, and the smooth, unblemished skin of an infant. He rinsed his mouth with the witch hazel and went to his bag, from which he removed a pair of green twill trousers and a short sleeve pullover shirt of the same new-leaf color. To these garments he added a pair of canvas running shoes, and over his bald head he fitted a wool watchcap, only slightly darker than the pants and shirt.

On the bed they had used, Gjertrud slept with a loose smile on her lips. As Croquet watched her she brought her arms up from beneath the covers, put her hands to her ears, and spun over so that all he could see was a tangle of blonde hair, a ginger-ale heap on the pillow. She said something, some muffled phrase that sounded to him like "F-Stop."

He picked up the leather jacket Sylvia had worn to Perry Street, murmured "Circles of confusion, Trood," and walked out of the door into the purpling day. He ambled away from the Inn office, along the side of the motel-building, and then around it and across the field which bordered the interstate freeway. Near it he turned south and moved through a grove of trees until he reached the exit ramp. Across from the bottom of the ramp was a closed gas station with a phone booth standing next to a collection of vending machines. He first called several numbers in New York City, each time hearing no more than ringing, ringing; finally, he asked for and got a number in Dallas and was pleased to hear the foggy, croaking voice of Decatur Samson.

"Decatur," he said, "wake yourself."

"Uh-oh," Decatur mumbled, "it's that time again. Whatsamatter, you need work?"

"I'm in the New England outback and, yes, I'm ready to travel."

"Swell, good. Would you like to play Caliban out in . . . where is it here? . . . Missoula, Montana? Starts rehearsals in three weeks."

"I'd rather Prospero," Croquet said.

"Part's filled. Besides, you fuck-up, I should de-Prospero you, take away your badge."

"That's enough of that," Croquet suggested. "I've got all these people here, in neat two-somes; even the Hollywood boy showed up, no thanks to you."

"Horsepucky," Decatur said, "I looked everywhere for the bugger."

Croquet coughed. "Well, he had his reasons for disappearing, I guess."

"Yeah," Decatur said, and after a pause, "Don't I hear the hot breath of the authorities? Just before I left Kennedy yesterday I saw the father of that Freeman girl being interviewed on the teevee. He said his daughter had been brainwashed and manipulated. That's a laugh."

"Sorrow, Decatur, I'll save for later. I need your help, one more time."

"I'm in Dallas, fool."

Croquet sighed. "Just consider my situation. I've got the California women and their men, one of whom is uhh . . . peculiar; the other, the jealous one, ought to be sent on a long trip *away* from his fugitive wife. O, and I have the beauty from the Riviera."

"Miss Nikon."

"Yes. I brought her along to keep her quiet, and now she's in my bed . . . again."

"Poor boy," Decatur said sadly. "What ever will you do?"

"The California ladies will go to Canada; they have to. The husband can stay in his garage and plead innocent to their whereabouts; and I'll take Miss Nikon on a long flight to Galapagos."

"The red head?"

Croquet gritted his teeth. "I don't know, I just don't know what he might have done. I want you to call FBI head-quarters in New York City, pretend you're one of those rad-lib attorneys — say Charlie Glass — and tell them you're ready to negotiate the surrender of the two women seen running from the townhouse."

"This is gettin' pretty realistic," Decatur said. "But I'll do it."

"It's only a diversion, buy some more time. They won't believe it, but they'll have to check."

"And how do the women get to Canada?" Decatur asked. "I don't think they ought to go on public—"

"There's a man in town who'll do it to save his soul."

"Ah, won't you ever stop? You ought to at least *read* for the Caliban role."

"Don't fret," Croquet said, "I'll be there."

"Good, very good. See you, then, peckerwood. May your star rise."

"Goodbye, Decatur, and thank you."

When Croquet opened #7's door he encountered not the sleeping silence he had expected, but a small bedlam like the first day of rehearsal for a noisy and misunderstood play.

"Why, here he is, Robin Hood himself," said a male

160

voice from someone he could not immediately see — Nick.

Before him, Gjertrud was sitting up in bed, the sheet wrapped tightly around her breasts; she was staring with obvious sympathy at the large form of Bip Rattray, who was pacing the length of the room, from bathroom to dresser, like a person beset and in shreds. In the mirror above the dresser Croquet made out Sylvia leaning against a wall, and behind the door that he had just opened stood Nick Winnoe, ready to pounce. Croquet closed the door, touched Nick lightly on the shoulder by way of greeting, and said, "Good morning, I'm glad you all could join us."

"Listen to him!"

"Damned albino medicine man."

Minor rebellion in the air.

Bip came close to him and patted him none too gently on the cheek. Her nostrils were flared and she seemed to have a metronomic tic beneath one liquid eye.

"Where is my Stanley?" she said. "I want you to tell me straight and I want you to tell me right now."

Gjertrud was reaching to the bedside table for her camera. "Trood," Croquet muttered, and she snapped her fingers away from the instrument and smiled weakly at him. Bip's eyes were still hard upon him, unblinking and — he realized — fearful.

"I'm worn out with this monkeybusiness," she said.

Nick crossed behind Croquet and sat on the made bed, while Sylvia remained slouched tensely against the wall, her eyes fixed on Bip. Croquet knew he had to pull out of this pause or risk an explosion; he removed his watchcap and let them all have the full force of his actual, shaved self: none had ever seen it save Gjertrud. Did Sylvia's lip curl just a touch? Nick sniffed heavily.

Croquet said, "I brought him to you last night, Bip."

"You did that," she said loudly, "and he was hopped to his precious little earlobes. Babbling away, jive this, jive that . . . narcs and phone numbers, I don't know what all, but you sure messed with his head, Mister." Her dark face had come closer to his own, so close a fleck of spittle from her mouth flew onto his cheek.

"Bip," Sylvia said, stepping toward her and putting an arm around her shoulder, drawing her away from Croquet's space. To him, the room was beginning to fill with invisible, panic-making gas; there was no need for this, at all.

"So he didn't stay the night with you?" he asked Bip.

She bared her teeth.

"Tell him," Sylvia said. "It can't hurt. Maybe it's not Mungo's fault."

Nick lighted a cigarette and blew the smoke in the direction of Croquet's head.

"Yeah," Bip said reluctantly. "He did settle down after a while, and it was nice, him paying attention to *me* instead of consulting the devils in his head. Then, in the midst of foolin' around on the bed he jumps up like a fright and says, 'I gotta get that *dog!*' And he starts leaping into his clothes. Well, I tackled him on the floor — enough was enough — and managed to haul him back in bed, where he settled down and performed with real . . . care. It was great, you know, and I felt redeemed of all this shit we've gone through, and we went to sleep as easy as can be." She closed her eyes for a moment, then popped them wide: "But when I wake up this morning he's gone, and I am concluding that it ain't nobody's fault but *yours.*"

Croquet smiled with all the force he could muster; with Bip calmed, all the others should fall into line like kids playing at soldier. "No, it's not," he said.

"Who then?" Nick asked, speaking for the first time since the sardonic Robin Hood remark, and now obviously with belligerence.

Croquet raised his hands in ignorance. "I can't be responsible for the effects of chemicals and fear. Stanley's a free man, free to follow dogs, ducks—"

"Goats like you," Nick interrupted, gazing directly at Sylvia, who still held tight to Bip.

"Look," Croquet said reasonably, "let's all go on out to the house of Eaton and find that dog of his. Where Jep is Stanley is."

162

"Are you serious?" Sylvia asked, letting go of Bip.

"Why not? We'll find him, surround him with benevolence, cure his latest obsessions."

"And Blount?" Nick said. Unexpected question.

Croquet shrugged. "Just waiting in the wings, Nicky baby," he said out of the side of his mouth.

"You know what," Gjertrud said gayly from the bed, "you people shouldn't do this before breakfast; it puts a strain on the brain. I'm so hungry I could eat Tommy with honey."

Croquet could hear the mood break. Good for Gjertrud.

"So it's a normal country Sunday?" Nick croaked.

"Not to me," Bip said. "I'm not letting you out of my sight, whitey, not until I've got Stanley back. You hear me, you *bat*."

Croquet nodded.

"No," Sylvia said, smiling sadly, speaking as if by rote, "not a bat . . . a man with blood on his head."

Now Gjertrud rose, still wrapped in her sheet, "So let's eat," she said. "The whole bloody menagerie can feed on roast dog. Or shall we send out for Chinese?"

In the midst of them all Croquet stood like a sinewy plant, receiving the burst of their motley colors, thinking that, finally, the unstable mechanisms were set in gear, and soon he could get back to work. O, how he hoped.

"Bagels and rue for the rutting griffin," said Nick into the mirror as Croquet — bald Possum Killer — replaced his watchcap and turned to lead them all from the crowded room.

CHAPTER TEN

What's it to ya, Moby Dick?

New England
May 3, 1970

BLOUNT'S Sunday began with the sensation that he was
alone in bed. You could see him stretch his legs into Sara's
territory, enjoying the space but at the same time regretting
its emptiness. Though he pulled the blanket up over his head
he could not regain the strenuous and purposeful world of
dream. He had to content himself with flashcards of the day
ahead: a variety of matters that ranged from the practical
(Jesus, schoolwork) to the sublime (Sara) to the disturbing
(Croquet) to the absurd (Stanley) to the ornery (Pablo) to
the domestic (Oliver and Tom) to the sympathetic (Nick and
Sylvia) to the necessary (exercise!) to ancient art (the proofs
of THINGS BURST) to the sexual (Sara); and with this last
came the knowledge that he had to pee. And so he carried
his useless erection into the bathroom and eliminated it from
his hodgepodge of problems and situations and tasks, none of
which seemed at all real until he was standing before the
mirror ready to begin shaving.

And even then he absorbed himself in the ritual rather than reflect or ponder or examine; he would simply *do* things. The razor did for the stubble but left an occasional trickle of lazy blood that he daubed and staunched with bits of toilet paper. Afterwards, he dashed his face with water, dried off, applied the witch hazel with a loud "Ahh," and combed his hair in some reasonable Sunday fashion. He thought he looked familiar. He left the bathroom humming "I've got a loverly bunch of coconuts," off-key, and in the bedroom he put on a pair of jeans and a T-shirt and his old cross-country shoes, then wandered out to the kitchen to find out what was up. Which was nothing at all. The counters on either side of the sink were clear and gleaming clean, as though his family had never passed through. He opened the refrigerator and found little more than a dreg of juice and a container of cottage cheese.

It was 10:30, he noted as he drank up the chemically sour orange juice. Out the kitchen window there was no one, and when he started out the door to see if the car was gone, he spied — stuck onto the small bulletin board next to the telephone — a note in Sara's elaborate handwriting:

MY LOVE,

WE'VE GONE TO HAVE BRUNCH
AT THE EATONS'. IF YOU GET
THE PAPER WE NEED EVERYTHING.

xxx SARA

Blount accepted the "brunch" part of the note: his family could follow their whims to the end of the ends of the earth, for all he would get excited. However, he did feel some anxiety about riding the battered bicycle down into town, as if accident or ambusher might await him at each and every crossroads. His fragile mood — jokey and cool, he knew —

carried him feinting and dancing to the hall closet, where he took down the wine-stained knapsack and slid it over his back, then went along out of the house, found his bike, and set off for town.

He rode easily, taking advantage of every slope, liking the sun and the smell of fresh-disced earth. As he came abreast of Fellows' Orchard, the apple trees seemed surrounded by a ruby haze, fainting from the shock of spring. He saw no vehicles, no dogs, no people, until he came up on the store, where a single white sedan was parked parallel to the gas pumps. A ways up the highway, at Alvin Marsh's garage, he could just make out Nick's pickup, which might have struck him as odd, but he was determined that on this day he would not be *struck* by anything.

Inside, he roamed the aisles until he had collected an armful of bread, butter, eggs, juice, ham, milk. And from the clerk he asked for and received his paper and a half-pound of store cheese. In front of the stack of papers from Boston, Manchester, and New York was a man dressed in green and an inappropriate woolen cap, with a skin remarkable for its lack of any color whatsoever. As Blount stuffed his goods into the knapsack, the man came toward him, picking up a box of doughnuts on the way, and as he drew close, said "Howdy," in a neutral voice.

Blount nodded and moved past the fellow to the door. "See you," he called to the clerk, and was surprised to hear the stranger say something like "Not if I see you first," but Blount kept on moving — none of that shit — until he had safely reached his bicycle. He placed the newspaper across the underslung handlebars and, holding it down with his thumbs, pedaled off home. When he turned right to go up to the orchard he saw that the Winnoe pickup was gone. The way home was uphill and he rode hard, conscious of the heavy weight at his back.

Once in the house, he prepared a breakfast and sat with it and the newspaper at the table in the living room. The sunlight dappled his eggs and cast a swathe across the front page, on which he found no reference to any matter that might

affect his personal history. Between bites of scrambled egg
he flipped idly through the pages of the first section, his eyes
roaming over the checkered columns until he discovered what
he almost subliminally had been looking for:

TWO SOUGHT IN
TOWNHOUSE BOMBING

Police and FBI officials reported yester-
day that they were still seeking Elaine
Freeman and an unidentified black wom-
an, the two who were seen fleeing from
the Perry Street townhouse which was
wrecked by explosions on May 1, and in
which three as yet unidentified corpses
were discovered by firemen.

Miss Freeman, 22, is the daughter of
Lionel Freeman, the owner of the town-
house which is believed to have been a
bomb factory for . . .

To the right of the column was a photograph of Elaine Free-
man: a pleasant, innocuous face — thick neck, heavy jaw,
neat hair — like a graduation photograph from an eastern
women's college, and one that did not bear any resemblance
to Sylvia Winnoe.

Blount hit the table a whack with the flat of his hand.
The entire tragic charade had toppled comically into place
before him, in his own backyard as it were, and now he be-
lieved he knew exactly what was what. He'd won by waiting;
these people hidden about his town would have plenty of
leisure to engineer their escapes from the obviously far-off
clutches of Law and Order. No Rule of Law had been upheld:
no good citizen (himself) had done his bounden duty: only
the politics of accident and shambles and misunderstanding
and comic self-importance had obtained. Such is the random-
ness of the world, he thought, and now, for him, normal life

could and would resume, as soon as the countryside was cleared of misfits and victimized women. Christopher Blount, finishing his eggs and turning to the Book Review, felt triumphant and used at the same time.

After he had washed his dishes and set the kitchen to rights, he searched through the record collection kept in the sideboard, and finally discovered a scratched and finger-printed copy of Moussorgsky's "Pictures at an Exhibition," which he put on the turntable, waiting for the slow, almost lackadasical phrases of introduction. While the music traveled forward, Blount fetched his proofs from the workroom and brought them to the living room, where he sat in the easy chair with a blue pencil and proceeded to fiddle with sentences and paragraphs he had written so long ago that they seemed the work of an ironical, precocious adolescent with a fondness for the nomenclature of breasts and for situations that, having reached the limit of comic potential, invariably took one more step. Yet Blount's Sunday mood provided a screen of tolerance, of whispered pride even, as he worked through the curling pages, unconsciously following the increasing tempo of Moussorgsky until he came to the last, the very last word. Meticulously, he corrected a "wouldn't" to a "would" in the smeary margin, and rested.

After a while he renewed his coffee, flipped the record, and searched the room until he found the envelope in which the proofs had arrived from New York. With some difficulty he crammed the pile into the container, sealed it with paper tape, and addressed it to the man who would see to the rest of the process: the quick execution of object and colorful wrapper; he shuddered with the suspicion that the eventual bookjacket would depict a contemporary chap with his crotch bizarrely askew; and then the slow burial across the country as reviewers struggled to explain how the ambiguous hope at the novel's end could possibly redeem the relentless comic sickness that had preceded it. But, goddamit, there were no puerile giggles in this one, no idealistic metaphors; in fact, no metaphors whatsoever; the book itself was that: THINGS BURST.

He threw the packet onto the sideboard and, scrutinizing the empty backyard through the window behind the table, he told himself that the next one — wherever it might be ahead of him — would run after the truth in a way controlled and clear-sighted, in a way that would cancel out the bile that he had burned yesterday afternoon in the 50-gallon drum. You can change your life; you can put love on the page; you are not inviolate and always in control; you can write words that support the contract of love between two, between four, between three . . . The music ended with a single phrase that referred back to its beginning.

He took the jumprope from its hook by the fireplace and skipped double-time to raise a sweat on his brow, in celebration of his deliverance from the chaotic soup. There was enough cockiness and control from his quickened metabolism that he didn't miss a beat when he noticed Nick Winnoe standing in the kitchen watching him, his arms akimbo, his face tense and gloomy . . . until the man threw up his hands and laughed outright, a deep hoarse laugh that Blount hadn't heard since he met him on the road to Bristol West.

"You're incorrigible, Blount!" he called out, and Blount ceased his efforts, but not before managing the trick of crossing the rope into a figure-eight and skipping right on into a blur. Then he did stop, controlling his breathing. Nick's features returned to glumness.

"You've seen the paper?" Blount asked, intending encouragement and sympathy.

"Do I need to?"

"There's nobody, nobody looking for Sylvia," Blount claimed. "You're safe."

"It's temporary," Nick said.

Blount seized a deep breath and said, "Have some coffee and tell me about it."

Nick looked baffled. "You've got a funny hair up your ass. But okay, I will have a cup."

Blount brought him a mug. "Where's Sylvia?"

Nick scowled, squinted out the window.

"I take it you've met my friend, the immortal Croquet,

also known as Thomas Wicket and Edmund Silver?" he asked.

"Some fool disguised as Angela Davis did pay me a visit last night. He seemed harmless enough."

Nick's sneer had nothing to do with Blount's light joke. "The fucking goat!" he said, his teeth clenched.

Blount was genuinely taken aback. "What am I hearing? Jealousy?" he asked.

"Cuckoldry," Nick muttered, and then turned from the window and smiled slightly. "I really didn't think I cared, you know, but all the parts of my body south of my nose seem to disagree violently. I've even told Sylvia, flip as can be, that it was okay . . . a harmless roll in the hay with that iguana. But it's not so, not so. I think I'm going to kill him." So saying, Nick blew off the steam from his coffee and took a noisy swig.

"What were you doing with him in the first place?" Blount asked, hoping to make a large detour around the killing-declaration.

Nick struck his forehead lightly with the tips of his fingers. "How can I answer that?" he said. "Why do you write? Why don't you have any friends? The man is genuinely fascinating, that's all."

"That's real helpful," Blount said.

"Shit. Mungo just arrived one day and we were hooked. From then on he was always *there,* delightfully I have to say, sort of part-way between what we were really doing and what we dreamed we were doing. If things constantly fell apart, nobody ever seemed to blame him." Nick put down the coffee cup. "I don't want to understand him, I just want to get rid of him."

"How?"

"I think he's a coward; if you push on him just right he'll melt, or fizzle, or fly away," Nick said, not sounding so sure.

"And then?"

"I'll have Syl to myself, and we can deal with the world without his mumbo-jumbo. On our own. But with your help, Chris."

Blount's curiosity couldn't prevent the old tic: "Wait a

minute," he said quickly.

"No, you wait," Nick injected. "I know you've been toyed with and all that, but I'm not following the script anymore. All I want is for you to help Sylvia and Bip get out of here, out of this country, away from the manhunt that's going to come down when those people in New York discover that the Freeman girl is right there in the morgue."

Blount looked at Nick for several beats; the other man's eyes were his own.

"All you have to do," Nick went on, "is drive the women to Montreal. I'll spend a month somewhere else, and then fly to Canada and join them. That should throw off the FBI pretty good."

"It's too simple," Blount said. "There has to be more to it. The other people . . . " His voice trailed off.

"Not to worry. Stanley's nuts, yes, but one way or another he and Croquet can be made to cancel each other out, like goddamned shades with opposite charges, vanishing ghosts. The Eatons are my friends; in fact, you'd like old Pablo if you'd give him a chance. And Monica, she's your own private problem."

"I can handle that," Blount said, despite a twinge of uncertainty in his intestines. "But what now?"

Nick spun around on one foot and ended up gazing at the painting over the fireplace. "Let's go to Pablo's, a Sunday drive. When we get there'll we'll shoulder through the crowds as we did on Friday. We'll speak to the children, and to my wife whom I believe you like, and I'll introduce you to Bip who is really wonderful despite her boyfriend; and after Lucia has fed us we'll take on the villains and rub them out. Poof!"

"Nice fairy tale," Blount said, smiling because Nick was so obviously enjoying his fantasy.

"Maybe so," he said. "But I tell you, something's bound to happen, and there's even a funny dame who'll take pictures of it."

By 11:30, Nick and Blount had mounted the maroon pickup and were on their way to Bristol West. Nick drove purposefully, with both hands on the heavy black wheel, but not fast; he seemed calm, almost serene, if such was possible for such an unsubtle and physical man. Blount hung one elbow out of the window and smoked one of Nick's Camels, enjoying the harsh bite of the smoke as it struck the back of his throat and invaded his lungs. Over the tappings and growls of the engine, Nick was singing something that sounded like the anvil chorus from "La Traviata," beating his hand on the door panel for the sound effects.

"Don't you ever leave this town?" Blount asked him when the large voice lapsed into silence.

"I might ask you the same question," he replied, "but in your case the answer doesn't matter; you've got a family enclave, and until recently it was safe. I came here sixteen months ago, after they told me Syl had been sentenced. And ever since, all I did was write silly filmscripts and work for Alvin. Mungo would keep me in touch with the real world, with little success, but on one occasion I did set out for Boston, and, you know, I got as far as Brattleboro and I became terribly afraid. Paralyzed. I turned back and haven't left since. It's a phobia, I know, but quite real."

"Then how do you expect to get to Canada?" Blount asked.

"No problem. Syl's out of prison, isn't she? So am I."

"Oh," Blount said, stubbing out his cigarette in the ashtray. Without much thought, words began to roll from his mouth. "I had an uncle like that over in New Hampshire; he never could travel more than sixteen miles from the town where he taught for twenty-nine years. They called him Alex the Rose because, as a substitute for all the traveling he missed, his chosen profession was the seduction of a great many of the town's wives. Once he had selected a target, he would learn her habits, and then one day when she was alone, he'd let himself into her house carrying a slim bunch of fresh roses. They say it worked one time out of three, and he was such a sweet man that no hue or cry ever got raised in all those years.

At Alex's funeral there must have been half a hundred cuck-olds, of every age and persuasion."

Nick lifted both hands from the steering wheel and crowed. "By god, Chris," he said, letting his hands fall with a wallop, "you've finally told me a story, shared a real fucking story. Thanks, thanks a lot!"

Blount came as close to being embarrassed as he had been in years, but so what? He joined his own laughter to Nick's. If they couldn't rise above the situation to come, make it turn out acceptably, they might as well both retire to Windsor and spend the rest of their lives fraternally whittling in front of the store.

The truck made the turn past the Congregational Church, where Blount used to water himself and where now he saw, beside the water faucet, a white car with New York plates, the same he had seen by the gas pumps earlier this morning. So the green man was the one; Blount's heart did a small dance of anticipation as they went slowly up the hill to Eaton's place. The *déjà vu* of Friday's picnic hit him forcibly: he could even see children over by the duck pond, but no adults in evidence as Nick took them up the driveway and parked the pickup.

Nick switched off the engine and flexed his fingers. "I appreciate our rapport," he said, "but maybe we better change gears here. I suspect everything inside will seem quite normal — a pleasant Sunday gathering. Mungo will try to convince you that it's all been a game, a joke that got out of hand, and he'll try to welcome you into the fold. And then that Gjer-trud will snap a group photo and we'll all go home feeling warm and convivial. Don't you believe it. Keep your eyes on the albino and his little sidekick, and when you least ex-pect it you'll see the shit hit the fan."

Blount started to ask him what *form* this might take, but his trust of Nick was such that he merely said, "Okay," open-ed his door, and finished with, "A little melodrama never hurt anybody."

No one came to greet them. They left the warmth of the outside and went into the kitchen.

Lucia Eaton stood in front of a black grill that had been placed over two burners on the cook stove; on the grill were several brown-speckled rounds of pancake, and beside the grill, on a plate, a stack of them several inches high. Her face was grim, Blount supposed, because of the work. He and Nick slouched into the room and made their hellos. Nick walked next to her and stood embracing her shoulders and gazing down at the pancakes.

"Looks real good," he said easily.

She sniffed and wiped her nose with a fist that held a spatula.

Blount noticed that the kitchen had suffered little else since his visit the evening before. Here and there were slumped packages of this or that, bowls, empty juice glasses. In the stillness he sensed that the house was empty.

"I'll feed you guys when I've done the others," Lucia said.

"Don't worry about us," Nick said. "Chris has eaten, I think, and my appetite can wait."

Blount paced a circle about the kitchen in an effort to contain his eagerness to find out what was going on in the backyard. Nick turned his head, still gripping Lucia, and winked at him.

Suddenly Lucia gave a low wail and buried her face against Nick's chest. "Pablo says we're going to Mexico," she snuffled.

Oh brother, Blount said to himself, preparing to leave the room.

Nick laughed. "So what's he want, to get closer to the mummies; watch a real revolution being stomped?"

"Nick! He just wants to take pictures, but Issy is *not* going to live in that filthy place."

"Oh, it's not so bad," Nick said. "Just another police state, only everyone seems too relaxed to make it work right."

"Who cares?" Lucia whimpered.

Blount picked up a fat tomato and began tossing it from palm to palm, back and forth with a rich slapping sound, while Nick murmured comfort at Lucia. As Blount tossed

174

he looked idly at his biceps as they emerged from the T-shirt and felt sure he could take any man on the place. Nick might have read this childish thought, for he released Lucia and in a flash of hand grabbed the tomato from the space of air between Blount's palms.

"Well, Lucia," Nick said, "I'm sorry you folks are leaving."

"That's fine for you to say," she cried, gesturing impatiently with the spatula and looking sadly at the floor until there was a carbon stink of pancakes burning. "Shoot," she said, and began to flip the cakes off of the griddle and onto the plate. "Why don't you go out back with the rest of them. There's enough women out there to give Pablo a hernia."

"What?" Blount asked, his first noise.

"Your Sara, Nick's wife, Monica, and the snotty one from New York with the camera, and—" Her voice fell. "— a black woman who's very mad." Lucia reached for a gallon tin of maple syrup.

"A real crowd of quiff," Nick said lightly, motioning with his head that he and Blount should go.

"Wait," Blount said. "What about the men?"

She poured the black-pitch syrup slowly into a pitcher. "What do we need men for, Chris? When we've got you two." Her voice was surprisingly bitter. "Just go get rid of Croquet."

"Let up, Lucia," Nick said blithely. "We'll tell Pablo Mexico isn't such a good idea."

"Don't patronize me." She was quite pissed-off. "If you really want to do something for me, you'll take Pablo's pistol there—" She nodded toward a holster hanging on a beam above her head. "—and shoot that bald fucker."

"Yeah," Nick said, either humoring her or trying to calm her down, Blount didn't know which. "Like shooting a Texas blind snake."

"He's about as blind as I am," Lucia said fiercely. "He gives me the willies and he scares Issy."

"Issy?" Nick said.

"When he looks at her she cries."

Nick stood quite still, his hands in the flapping back

pockets of his stained pants. "Stanley? His pal isn't here?"

Lucia picked up the platter and the pitcher. "No. Maybe he's off with the goddamn dog. Come on out and join the party."

It was a curious sight, Blount thought as he stood in the frame of the back door and gazed across the patch of grass that lay between him and the crude table that had been set up on sawhorses, in sunlight. A banquet. Lucia set down the brunch in front of Pablo, who sat at one end of the table like an aging bandit leader in his sleeveless vest and red bandana. Next to him, on his right, was a cool and pleasant Monica; on his left, her back to Blount, was Sara, taller by far than anyone else at the table. Next to her he saw the bowed, bright head of Sylvia Winnoe, and across the way, next to Monica, was Bip, who didn't look so much angry as out-of-place, as she stared at the man who sat opposite Pablo: Mungo Croquet. For Blount, the scene was transformed to the realm of the harmless by his realization that the six brunchers were being solemnly photographed by a golden-haired woman in a silk blouse who stood away from the table, working with a camera that blinked and shone in the sun: family life in New England.

Blount left the door to join this discreet celebration and followed Nick across the lawn. He positioned himself behind Sara with his hand on her shoulder, listening vaguely to the greetings from the people at the table. He saw, down the hill at the duck pond, the figures of children. There was the Eaton girl in pink. And Oliver, holding a long stick. Tom, hanging back with his thumb in his mouth. They were all looking across to the woods that led to the cemetery. There were no ducks to be seen.

Pablo was saying, ". . . and I believe you've met that man there, Mungo Croquet of New York City."

Blount nodded politely to Bip and moved past Sylvia until he had come close enough to Croquet to see his peaceful pink eyes.

"You've changed," Blount said, putting out his hand; he would play this correctly. As their skin touched, Blount became conscious of two things: that the woman had knelt to photograph the moment; and that Croquet's skin was as cold as the ice he'd dreamed of the night before — a cold more known than actually felt.

"My street clothes," Croquet drawled. He cocked his ivory head to the right. "This is Gjertrud."

She rose gracefully to her feet, allowed the camera to swing down to her chest, and said, "Nice to see you, Christopher. I like your work, very much."

Unreal gathering!

While Blount faced Gjertrud he sensed that behind him at the table, where Nick must by now have seated himself, a hush was blooming. As he spoke to Gjertrud this was underscored by the sharp sounds of plates, forks, coffee cups sipped and replaced on the board.

Blount decided that Gjertrud was being sincere as she said, "I'd like to do the jacket photo for your new book; your wife says you don't have one."

"All right," he said evenly. "See what you can do. It's called THINGS BURST."

Someone asked if he wanted coffee.

He turned and shook his head, saw Lucia disappearing into the house carrying an empty pot. Gjertrud sat down next to Croquet; her fingernails were black, as black as Nick's.

He wouldn't sit himself; the view from above was better. As the hush lengthened, he knew something was going to happen; he knew it as surely as he knew he would come out of it with his heart and head intact.

"So what's going on with you?" Croquet asked him from below.

"Oh," Blount said finally, having affirmed a certain humorous power in the fact of his standing. "Strange arrivals, accidents, dreams. I do my work and I'm safe."

"Is that right?" Croquet said, with a mouthful of pancake and syrup.

Blount glanced away from Croquet, down the length of the table where he could see Pablo talking with the good

177

Monica; Bip staring straight ahead and chewing as if her very life depended upon the present sustenance; Gjertrud self-contained and glittering. He heard Nick smacking his lips.

"You know, Chris," Nick said, "whitey there might as well be shot for cuckoldry and shamanism."

His laugh was like breaking wind among gentry. No one moved.

Until Croquet jostled his chair back from the table's end, crossed one knee over the other, and took a slow sip of coffee. "Is *this* your problem, Nicky?"

The time had come. A simple action could destroy this picture forever. Blount knew it. He casually bent at the waist, reaching down for Croquet's hanging foot, which he seized and pulled up, causing the bald albino to rock back in the chair and tumble with it to the ground, still in a sitting position but now confused, irritated and possibly hurt, all at once.

Fakery dumped!

There were hands on Blount's bunched shoulder muscles, and Sara whispered into his ear, "Oliver knows."

Blount turned his head and looked at her. Her face was calm, though fear lines ran like small cracks from her eyes. "He knows what?"

Sara didn't answer, but instead raised her head coolly — aloofly — and said to Croquet: "Listen, your little seance is over. Of all people, you should know when it's time to exit. My son tells me your friend is down in the cemetery, so why don't you go get him . . . and then leave us, just go back where you came from."

Croquet was looking up at them with an expression so contracted and intense that Blount could only read it as pain, or a stymied and awful concentration. Nothing happened.

Blount looked around for Nick and saw him moving for the back door, but he was stopped there by Lucia and her burden of pancakes. She blocked the door with her thick body. Blount would remember thinking that the ludicrous, never-to-be-used gun could well have been stuck into the waist of her shorts, but he never knew if this was true, never had to know, for at that moment came a high-pitched shout from the pond, "DADDY!"

And the tableau broke into fragments. Croquet gathered himself and performed a neat and gymnastic backwards flip out of his grounded chair. After landing on his feet he began to skip sideways toward the pond. In the mass and flutter of movement, Blount saw Nick begin to run after him; Sara, too, started for the pond, while Bip stood and slowly turned away from the table. Then Monica had by-passed Blount and snatched the camera from around Gjertrud's neck . . . by its strap she spun it like an ancient slingshot, then let it loose so that it arced high and twinkling in the air between the table and the pond below. Sylvia stepped quickly between Nick and Croquet, stopping Nick's forward rush with an arm that seemed to Blount as fragile as a twig.

Croquet kept skipping backwards, downhill, his body supple under the green stuff of the costume.

Another cry, this time a girl's, "LOOK!"

Blount saw that they were all staring, that what they saw, what he saw, was Stanley Fielding come out of the cemetery woods on the other side of the pond from where the children were gaping.

Stanley's hair was the color of flame, his arms were spread wide, and he was naked. He was shouting something Blount couldn't make out; shouting, beckoning, and then he lowered his arms and stood very still for a moment. The arms fluttered, fluttered faster and faster, until Stanley's entire body began a graceful flapping that caused his distant and innocent member to waggle at them all, at the adults, at the children, at skipping Croquet, at Blount, whose simple desire for pursuit came over him like a fainting spell. He began to run downhill, sensed Nick behind him, could still see the red-smudged penis making its far-off semaphore: a message that would never need de-coding.

Croquet, several yards away, between Blount and the pond, suddenly wheeled and began to sprint, straight for the water, straight for the children. Women's voices rose in the air behind Blount — Bip's the loudest — as he increased his speed. In pursuit of order. In pursuit of family. In pursuit of love. In pursuit of himself.

What happened then was not possible. Croquet's flashing green legs reached the edge of the slimy water; the children had stood apart, forming a kind of portal through which he passed; he went through it and leapt into the air, his legs continuing to pump madly, and carrying him the full width of the pond. Impossible. But Blount saw it happen, saw him land in front of Stanley, heard the sound of Croquet's tennis shoes smack and suck at the spongy earth, saw Stanley embrace Croquet like a longlost lover, saw the two of them break apart, and, joined only at the hands, turn toward the house and bow, with dignity and grace. Then, you could see quite clearly, they turned and faded — not fled, not melted, not disappeared — faded into the cemetery woods like shades, like shades going home, like shades going to find a lost ghost-dog in the woods. And it was at that moment that Blount, at full tilt, tripped over the stick Oliver was holding and fell fullface into the cool stuff at the pond's edge, surrounded by children.

At precisely two o'clock p.m., on May 3, 1970, a Sunday, Christopher Blount kissed his boys, embraced his wife's lover Monica (their babysitter), and set out in his red sedan for Canada. In the backseat of the car were Bip Rattray and Sylvia Winnoe, while in front, with him, was his wife Sara Leary Blount, who all the way to the border kept an eye on her cautious husband at the wheel.